The Christology of Rudolf Steiner

The Christology of Rudolf Steiner

Exploring the Spiritual Reality at the Heart of Christianity

Willem Frederik Veltman

Floris Books

Translated by Philip Mees

Most quotations from the New Testament are taken from *The New Testament: A Version by Jon Madsen*, which follows Rudolf Steiner's indications on Bible texts and translations. Old Testament quotations are taken from the New International Version (NIV). Where some New Testament passages have been taken from the NIV this is indicated.

First published in Dutch as *De spirituele werkelijkheid van het Christendom*
by Uitgeverij Vrij Geestesleven, Zeist in 1996
First published in English by Floris Books, Edinburgh in 2026

Also available as an eBook

Authorised EU Representative: Easy Access System Europe,
Mustamae tee 50, 10621 Tallinn, Estonia gpsr.requests@easproject.com
British Library CIP data available
ISBN 978-183575-014-8

Contents

Foreword

My decision to write a book about Christianity was not taken after long deliberation, but it did have a long build-up. More than fifty years ago I had a conversation with someone about the miracles in the gospels. I could not view these supernatural events as divine magic, for I was convinced that God would never do anything that goes against the laws of nature. Neither could I assume that these miracles were the pious fantasies of exalted followers or were regarded as being merely symbolical. The 'clever' explanation for how Jesus was able to walk on the sea – that he stood on a little board just below the surface of the water – only convinced me of the imbecility of intellectual opinions of the Bible.

There had to be, it seemed to me, an explanation that made the miracle accessible to the intellect but did not rob it of its significance.

Someone I knew at the time explained to me that the walking on the sea (Mt 14; Mk 6; Jn 6) was a supersensory experience the disciples had during the night. They were in their boat, which is a symbol for the transition from day to night consciousness. Following their experience of the so-called feeding of the five thousand on the banks of the

Sea of Galilee earlier that day, they became clairvoyant in their sleep and were able to behold Jesus in his spiritual form 'walking on the sea'. Fear seized them (contact with the divine always provokes fear in a person in the first instance) but when Jesus came on board they immediately landed – in other words, they woke up (Jn 6:21).

This explanation, which does not go against the laws of nature, and is also not symbolic but points to a real spiritual event, not only satisfied me completely, but also worked like an inner breakthrough. I knew this must be true, and that the source from which my friend had drawn this insight must be a source of truth. I did not need to leave my intellect behind in order to believe Christianity; I could understand it and still retain the full majesty of divine revelation. As a scientifically schooled person I could be a Christian without denying my need for insight and understanding. I could think in a modern scientific manner without having to apologise for trying to approach and understand the content of the gospels as a reality.

The source of truth I had come across was Rudolf Steiner's anthroposophy. My friend had given me the anthroposophical explanation of Jesus walking on water, and with this had given me a decisive experience of the truth.

Since that time, fifty years ago, I have immersed myself in Steiner's anthroposophy. I have been continually astonished that his insights, which really signify a renewal of Christianity, have not been taken up more extensively by the present culture. It is of course understandable that spiritual insights of such a revolutionary nature need time to become accepted. However, I am convinced that in our time there lives a strong need in many people to become acquainted with such refreshing views concerning Christianity.

With this book I hope to reach those who may not wish to plough through Steiner's entire work, but are nevertheless interested in learning something about his insights. For this reason, I aim to present a summary of Steiner's Christology as it is spread throughout his work. Completeness will certainly not be achieved, but in view of the inexhaustible nature of the subject it is also not the goal.

W. F. Veltman
March 1996

1

Faith, Knowledge and the Need for a New Revelation

Christianity, with its Jewish, Greek and Roman components, has formed the bedrock of Western culture for over a thousand years. Our calendar with its festivals of Christmas, Easter, Ascension and Pentecost, and the church steeples that dominate the landscape of Europe, are just a couple of examples of this. Many more things indicate the Christian nature of Western civilisation.

But in the twentieth century, when science and technology dominate our society, and a natural scientific view of the human being and the world excludes all consideration of the spiritual, can we really say that the essence of our culture is still Christian?

Some Christians often feel estranged from the origins of their faith. Many adherents either don't believe in the main doctrines of the church at all or at least have serious doubts about them, and they often disagree with ecclesiastical positions on questions concerning divorce, birth control and abortion. Many priests and pastors tell their followers that they don't always know what to think about such things either, but that it is good to keep with holy traditions and trust that

God knows what he's doing. There are echoes in this of the old saying *credo quia absurdum* – 'I believe because it is absurd'.[1]

There have been efforts to consider the role of Christian faith in contemporary society, but the changes that have arisen from such debates are only so much tinkering around the edges in an attempt to accommodate people's more modern attitudes. No comma or letter, let alone a word or sentence, of religious dogma has been changed.

Meanwhile, many young people are turning away from Christianity because it is too strongly tied to the past and so little focused on the future. Moreover, in an era of increasing individual freedom, asking people to believe what cannot be proven on the basis of authority alone, is untenable. What is known stands opposed to what is believed, and in the end what cannot stand up to intellectual enquiry is dismissed as untrue. Astute analyses and conclusions don't really throw new light on any part of the Christian faith.

But things were not always this way.

In the first centuries of Christianity the bearers of spiritual culture were not intellectuals but 'knowers' in a different sense. People at the time spoke about *gnosis,* a knowledge of spiritual realities obtained by individuals with clairvoyant abilities. The knowledge of these initiates, drawn from the ancient mystery cults, was gradually lost, however, and by the fourth century it had practically disappeared. In some cases, it has been deliberately eradicated. In the absence of this old wisdom, a need soon arose for these ideas to be explained, especially those concerning the nature of Jesus and the divine Trinity. There were diverging views and heated disagreements. Councils and dogmas were needed to instruct the faithful, but that led to a belief based on authority. In the Middle Ages, faith became a church-sanctioned state of mind, supported and maintained by ritual pomp and beautiful liturgical music.

Gradually, however, all of this had to give way to what would eventually become our modern culture, with its scientific knowledge that depends on empirical evidence and rational thinking. Faith was slowly banished from the field where material science was developing as the new knowledge. Medieval Christian philosophers began to speak of the 'double truth': the truth of faith and the truth of science, and because they might contradict each other, human beings should keep them separate.

This irrational mindset still predominates in Western culture. A child learns the creation story of Genesis in Sunday school and then during the week is taught the theory of evolution as formulated by Charles Darwin. On Sunday you have to 'believe'; during the week you are allowed to 'know'. For the child as they get older, the contradiction between these two worldviews quickly becomes a problem. When you add to this Protestant Biblical criticism, which has served to undermine the faith, Christianity appears to be a religion that is unable to justify its own existence.

It was necessary that faith, for a time, took the place of the old knowing, but that time is now also coming to an end. For Christianity to have any future, a new approach is needed based on spiritual insight and inner experience, one that provides insight into both the earthly and divine worlds, the human being, and perhaps most significantly of all, the incarnation of Christ.

The importance of this cannot be overstated. Many people of other races and cultures would be able to recognise the essential significance of Christ if the Christianity of today did not stand in the way. If the path could be cleared, if a new light could be thrown on what took place in the Holy Land two thousand years ago, then it might turn out that Christianity is not so much a religion like other great religions, but a central affair that concerns *all* of humanity. Not because of the content of a particular doctrine, but because of the actual reality of Christ's life.

One person who sought to develop such an approach was the Austrian philosopher and founder of anthroposophy, Rudolf Steiner. Steiner was born in 1861 in the small town of Kraljevec in what was then the Austro-Hungarian Empire but today is in Croatia. From an early age, Steiner was naturally able to see into the spiritual world, but he saw it as his life's task to develop a systematic way that would allow other people to bridge the gap between the world of the senses and the world of the spirit. As a student he found the seeds of such a spiritually oriented research method in the work of several Central European thinkers, foremost among them the German poet and scientist Johann Wolfgang von Goethe. Steiner went much further than his predecessors, however, creating a modern spiritual science that can be seen as building on and going beyond the natural science of our time.

Steiner's path of spiritual development consists in strengthening the normal soul faculties of thinking, feeling and willing through intensive exercises and meditations. These work on the spiritual senses that lie dormant and seedlike in all of us, thereby allowing us to awaken to higher spiritual worlds. There we can acquire supersensible knowledge about the world and the human being.[2] In the books he wrote and the many lectures he gave, Steiner sometimes used the phrase 'exact clairvoyance' to describe the method by which such spiritual research is carried out.[3]

An important source of supersensible knowledge is what is known as the Akasha Chronicle or the Akashic Record, which is found in a high spiritual realm that can only be approached by initiates, like Rudolf Steiner, who have developed their consciousness to the requisite degree. The Sanskrit word 'akasha' refers to a fine, spiritual substance in which is imprinted a record of everything that happens not only on earth, but also in the cosmos. These are preserved in spiritual pictures that are not static but full of life and movement, which often makes them difficult to understand.

Another challenge in reading the Akashic Record is being able to find what you are looking for in the first place. If we are searching for something in an ordinary book, then we often turn to the index (if it has one) at the back to find the page with the relevant information. With the Akasha Record it is much more difficult; it is not a book with pages, but a highly mobile sphere of gigantic size. The initiate must bring their own 'index' with them if they want to find something, some indication that will help them find what they are looking for.

Added to this is the fact that the pictures seen in the Akashic Record are not like a photograph of the event or person, but a kind of inner vision of them. The way someone moved, their gestures, the impulses of will that drove them to do certain deeds – all of this is what the initiate sees in the akasha. It is as though the person stands spiritually before them and speaks to them.

Such spiritual research underlies Rudolf Steiner's communications about the events in the Holy Land at the time of Christ. Sceptics like to claim that, in order to arrive at these communications, he interpreted the gospels in his own fantastic way and mixed all kinds of gnostic ideas into them. However, he did not base himself on traditional documents but penetrated into higher realms of consciousness where he could read the Akashic Record. Only after he had arrived at concrete results in his investigations did he take existing documents such as the gospels and compare their content with that of his spiritual experiences. The latter agreed to a surprising extent with the documents, indicating that both Steiner and the gospel writers must have drawn upon a common source. We will deal later with the apparent contradictions found in them.

Rudolf Steiner once said that if all the bibles in the world were destroyed, their contents could still be found again through spiritual-scientific research.

Not only did he find the content of the existing gospels through his independent spiritual research, he also found important facts that the gospels do not explicitly mention, or at least only hint at. As it turns out, the gospel writers composed their books like mystery scripture. The terminology they use, such as 'on the mountain', 'he came to him in the night', and other expressions, was familiar to those who still had connections with the ancient wisdom of the temple mysteries. But this wisdom was fading fast. Incorrect interpretations and errors in translation occurred already in the translation of the original Greek text into Latin (something else we will return to later). The gospels could still function as the source of the Christian faith, but no longer for a true knowledge of Jesus Christ.

Rudolf Steiner, however, was able to penetrate into the old mystery wisdom and contemplate the gospels in that light and in the light of a new spiritual knowledge. This makes an exegesis possible that does not lead to dogmatism, but to a free insight into the mysteries of Christianity in which the ancient mysteries are resurrected.

It is not at all my intention to claim, or even suggest, that the anthroposophical view of the Mystery of Golgotha – the term Steiner used to refer to the incarnation, death and resurrection of Christ – offers a definitive explanation. Later times will no doubt bring new, different insights, because the development of humanity will always bring further far-reaching revelations. In my view, it is exactly the mistake of traditional Christianity that it has trapped itself in dogmas and definitive statements.

For our time, Steiner's spiritual insights may be clarifying and convincing; in later times they will be broadened and deepened again. The core, which points to the objective deed of Christ, will stay. Its significance will ever again have to be conquered by human beings, because new perspectives will keep opening up. The author of the Gospel of John says at the end of his book:

> Jesus also did many other things, but if they were all written down one after another, I do not think the world itself could contain the books that would have to be written. (Jn 21:25)

What is important here is not only revelation through a new form of spiritual knowledge, but also the manner in which this revelation is accepted and taken in, namely by spiritualising our normal cognitive capacities. We must develop our thinking activity so that we can *think along with* these new revelations – that is the first step on the path towards experiencing these revelations for ourselves.

A new capacity to behold the spiritual world will be a normal human cognitive ability in the future, I have no doubt about that. We can see the first signs of it already. We are still living in a time of transition in which, together with new cognitive capacities, a new power of faith is also being prepared, which we could characterise with the words: *credo quia comprehensibilis,* 'I believe because I can comprehend it.' This comprehension is no intellectual hubris, but a reverent openness to the truth that reveals itself continually in ever new and far-reaching aspects during the course of human development.

2

What Preceded Christianity?

Christianity arose within a small group of people, most of whom were Jewish. Among the great cultures of antiquity, this people, small in number but possessing great inner strength, represented a peculiar exception. Whereas other tribes and peoples around them worshipped many gods, the Jewish people worshipped only one God. This monotheistic character was transmitted to Christianity, which led to Christians then and now to consider polytheism to be abominable. This prejudice, however, stands in the way of a proper understanding of Christianity.

The cultural impulse that began with the appearance of Jesus Christ in the Holy Land spread with unimaginable force across the Greek and Roman world (and further afield to Armenia, Central Asia, India and Ethiopia), and from there into north, west and central Europe. During the great migrations of the fifth and sixth centuries, Celtic and Germanic tribes converted to Christianity, followed later by Slavic, Finnish and Magyar tribes. The history of these European peoples was completely different from that of the Jews, Romans, Greeks, Egyptians and the other peoples of Asia Minor. The latter had produced great cultures over the course of thousands of years, with philosophy, poetry, art, music, sculpture and stunning architecture, all of which was brought to bear to explore and express this new religion.

Very little of this existed in the Germanic, Celtic and Slavic tribes, except for the poetry and music of their skalds and bards. We can perhaps see them as preparaing for a future culture of which they would be the bearers.

So what was it that allowed Christianity to be taken up by such a broad range of people at such different stages of cultural development?

The key to this lies in what existed before Christianity and helped to pave the way for it.

Just like the highly civilised cultures around the Mediterranean, the early northern European tribes possessed sources of wisdom from which not only religious but also daily social life was nourished, organised and maintained. These were the so-called mysteries, which had existed among all peoples and all races from ancient times. All religion, science and art originated from them, as well as social customs, festivals and even economic instruction. The mysteries differed from region to region depending on the nature and tasks of the different peoples, but they also had common characteristics – similar rites, and inner and outer connections that could be found in mutually related peoples.

Someone who found no satisfaction in outer religion, nor in the ordinary knowledge of the time, might go to one of the mystery temples in the hope of achieving deeper insight. If they were found worthy by the priests, then a period of strict preparation began. Secluded from the world, and leading an extremely ascetic life, the candidate for initiation – or *myste* – had to undergo all kinds of physical and psychic trials. Through meditative exercises and occult rituals they were prepared for initiation, which could only take place once they had overcome their lower nature and the bonds that tied them to earthly existence.

The spiritual world into which the *myste* tried to penetrate is of a completely different nature from the reality that surrounds us on earth. The *myste* worked on their feeling life in such a way that they underwent a complete inner transformation. This was accompanied by a profound crisis in which they endured terrifying experiences. It was like dying and journeying into the emptiness and darkness of the underworld.

When myths and sagas describe how the hero must make a journey into the underworld to fetch something rare or precious, or to save a virgin from the power of some obscure figure, it is always a picture of initiation. We know that only those will succeed who possess moral strength and purity such as the noble hero Hercules.

If the *myste* could endure the terror of the initiation trial and remain steadfast, then a new world opened up for them. Or rather, they themselves were reborn with the ability to see the world with the eyes of the spirit. The newly initiated *myste* now perceived the higher spiritual powers at work in the world that are hidden to the consciousness bound to the physical senses. They came to know the gods and the lower spiritual beings in nature, and these beings shared their knowledge and wisdom with the *myste*. They could look through the world of appearance, of life and death, and came to know, as a fact of their experience, the imperishable world of the spirit.

The initiate returned to their community a renewed human being, and they often went by a new name. The people around them knew nothing of what the initiate had experienced, and the initiate was bound by the strictest oath of secrecy not to reveal the mystery wisdom that had been imparted to them. The punishment for breaking this oath was death. It was also considered just as 'sinful' for the uninitiated to hear mystery secrets. For someone to learn occult truths for which they have not undergone a process of purification, it can have a destructive effect that ultimately works in an evil way. This is demonstrated by the Roman emperors who, without the proper moral preparation, forced the priests of the mysteries to initiate them into these truths. From that moment they were worshipped as gods, but they gradually became mentally unbalanced and exhibited extreme cruelty and destructive tendencies.

For the true initiate the common pictures of the gods lost their significance. They did not deny the existence of the popular deities, but they knew that the representations of them had been formed by the people themselves. After all, these gods often displayed the same characteristics that earthly human beings displayed. The initiate knew that behind these pictorial representations, handed down in myths, lay the true realm of the gods. But the initiate had also learned that this divine realm rests on an even greater power. Xenophanes of Colophon, the pre-Socratic philosopher of the sixth century BC wrote:

> One God is among the gods and among human beings
> the greatest.
> Not in gestalt, nor thought equal to moral beings.[1]

These words point to the 'hidden' God of the mysteries. No mortal eye nor mortal intellect can perceive or comprehend this highest God. Where can this God be found? He has, as it were, been absorbed into his own creation. He has sacrificed himself and divided himself among the myriad things of the world. Nature is the great grave of the Godhead. Only in the human being does the God still live, but without form. He must be awakened by human beings through their own activity.

The initiate therefore viewed themselves as an actor in the great world drama that released God from enchantment in the world. In *Christianity as Mystical Fact,* Rudolf Steiner describes the profound experience of God in the mysteries as follows:

> The *mystai* understood that 'God is love' in a special higher sense. For God has gone to the utmost lengths of love. He has sacrificed himself in infinite love, poured himself out, dismembered himself into the manifold things of nature. They live, but he is not alive in them; he slumbers in them, but comes alive in human beings who are able to experience the life of God within themselves. But if human beings are to attain this *gnosis,* they must creatively release it within themselves. Looking into their own being, they find the divine as a hidden creative power, not yet released into existence. Within the soul lies the place where the spellbound God may return to life.
>
> The soul is the mother who can receive the divine seed from nature. If the soul allows herself to be impregnated by nature she will give birth to the divine. Out of the marriage of the soul with nature the divine is born, no longer a 'hidden God' but something manifest, alive ... In human beings the spirit has been

> released from enchantment; yet it is the offspring of the spellbound God. He is not the great God who was, and is, and shall be, yet he may in a certain sense be taken as a revelation of him. The Father remains at rest in the unseen. The Son is born to human beings out of their own souls.
>
> Initiatory knowledge is thus an actual event in the cosmic process. It is the birth of the divine child – a process just as real as any natural process. The great secret of the *mystai* was precisely this, that they creatively release the divine child in themselves. First of all, however, they must be prepared so as to recognise it. The uninitiated know nothing of the Father of this divine child. The Father slumbers under a spell. The child seems to be born of a virgin, the soul giving birth to him without impregnation. Whereas all her other offspring are begotten by the world of the senses, and have a father who can be seen and touched in perceptible existence, the Son of God is uniquely begotten of the eternal, hidden Father himself.[2]

Steiner is clearly indicating here that there is a direct connection between the life of Jesus Christ as described in the gospels and the experiences initiates went through in the mysteries. This connection has also been identified in the study of ancient religion, for, vows of secrecy notwithstanding, a lot of information about initiation procedures can be found in Hellenistic literature.

But that is not the only similarity with the Gospel story. Many of the ancient mystery religions contain rituals of death and resurrection, such as the Adonis and Attis rites in Asia

Minor, and descriptions of a holy sacrificial meal are quite common too. We find them, for instance, in the Mithras mysteries from Persia. The mysteries of the Egyptian Osiris and the Greek Dionysus celebrate the birth of a Son God out of a godhead that has been torn apart and whose members are scattered throughout the world, sunk down in nature as in a grave. In these myths we encounter Isis and Persephone as personifications of the soul, both of whom give birth to a spirit child: Horus in the Egyptian myth and Iacchos in the Greek. The correspondence with Mary and the virgin birth in the gospels is evident.

In a grotto in Chartres, at a site where the crypt of the famous cathedral would later be, Druids worshipped the *Virgo Paritura*, 'the Virgin who shall bear a child'. The child she was expected to bring into the world was the coming Redeemer. The expectation of a World Saviour, a Son of God, was by no means limited to the Jewish people, but lived in all peoples of antiquity.

In the mysteries, the initiate experienced the birth of the Redeemer, of a higher divine Self, in their soul. They experienced this mystery as a personal enlightenment known as *epiphaneia*, meaning 'appearance' or 'manifestation'. However, the expectations were of one who would bring with them the higher Self of humanity as a whole. The mysteries pointed to this future saviour.

This 'pre-Christian' Christianity is represented in Greek philosophy and in many gnostic-esoteric sects and movements within Judaism and outside it.[3] When the evangelist John in the prologue to his gospel spoke about the divine Logos or Word, he was expressing what was already in his time an age-old doctrine of the three Logoi – which is none other than the ancient mystery knowledge of the divine Trinity dressed up in philosophical terminology. According to tradition, the pre-Socratic philosopher Heraclitus placed his book about the Logos in the temple of Artemis in Ephesus, which without a doubt means that it was a mystery book that could only be comprehended by initiates.[4]

In the philosophical writings of Plato countless passages testify to the influence of mystery knowledge,[5] and Socrates, the principal character in Plato's dialogues, lived and died as a Master who already in life had overcome everything earthly and sensory and lived in the light of the eternal spirit.[6]

In Plato's *Timaeus and Critias,* which contains a discussion of the origin of the world, we read that the Maker and Father of the All has poured himself out into the corporeality of the world. The world soul is bound to this world body in the form of a cross. Here again we encounter the thought that in nature the divine being is hidden as though imprisoned or under a spell, and only by the cognitive activity of the human being is it resurrected from this grave. In the wisdom-filled human soul the divine is reborn.

Special mention should go to the Jewish philosopher Philo of Alexandria, who was also an ardent Platonist.[7] The doctrine of the Logos occupied a central place in his work, and in his contemplations of the Second Logos he approached the character of the Christ-being so closely that it's surprising to consider that he must have been completely ignorant of the deeds of Jesus in the Holy Land, whose contemporary he was. It is tantalising to consider whether he would have recognised the Second Logos in Jesus Christ if he had actually met him.

Finally, we must briefly consider one of the many sects and religious communities that existed in the ancient world around the time of Christ: the Essene settlement at Qumran on the north-west shore of the Dead Sea. This came to academic and popular attention in the twentieth century with the discovery of the Dead Sea Scrolls, a collection of over nine hundred ancient manuscripts that included biblical texts, apocryphal writings and other Jewish literature.[8]

The Essenes were members of an apocalyptic Jewish sect who were preparing for the coming of the Messiah as mentioned by the great prophets. Related communities also existed in Egypt where they were called Therapeutae. According to Philo of Alexandria who wrote about them, they lived in secluded communities, and their way of life was defined by ascetism and a strict adherence to community rules and hard discipline. Without a doubt this was a path of initiation that aimed at the total purification of the inner person in order to awaken the god in their inner being.

Among the texts relating to the Essenes' Messianic beliefs are their expectation that *two* Messiahs would appear: a priestly Messiah of Aaron, representing the Levitical priesthood, and a kingly Messiah of Israel, descended from the House of David. We will come back to this later.

The Qumran scrolls also speak of a 'Teacher of Righteousness', a great initiate who lived about a hundred years before Christ and who was the spiritual leader of the communities spread over the Holy Land and Egypt. It is thought that this teacher is the same figure referred to in Talmudic writings as Jeshu ben Pandira – Jesus, the son of Pandira. This Jeshu ben Pandira was persecuted by King Alexander Jannaeus,[9] falsely accused of blasphemy and heresy, and eventually stoned to death. His body was hung on a tree.

Already in the second century AD Jeshu ben Pandira and Jesus of Nazareth were confused with each other. Jeshu ben Pandira is mentioned several times in the Talmud, but in both later Jewish and Christian theology these passages were misinterpreted as relating to Jesus of Nazareth. This error has caused many people to ignore the historical event that centres on Jesus Christ, and which is of a totally different order than the execution of the leader of a sect considered by fanatical rabbis to be a heretic. But it has also meant that the importance of the figure of Jeshu ben Pandira has likewise been overlooked.

On the basis of his spiritual-scientific research, Rudolf Steiner was able to throw light on the Teacher of Righteousness as one of the great initiates who, through the Essenes and the Therapeutae, prepared people for the coming of the Messiah.[10] In this connection it is understandable that John the Baptist and also Jesus of Nazareth himself had close contacts with the Essenes.

The confusion of Jesus of Nazareth with the Teacher of Righteousness, and more broadly between ancient mystery practices and the gospels, have led people to cast doubt on the life of Christ and everything connected with it.

Enlightened theologians and academics explain these correspondences by assuming that a new sect emerged in the Holy Land (the members of which were initially called Galileans or Nazarenes and only later Christians) that drew upon the ancient mysteries to invent the fable of Jesus' life, death and resurrection. The doctrine of Christianity would in that case be merely a put-together product in which mythological, mystical and philosophical ingredients, mixed with Judaism and Buddhist teachings of compassion and love, were combined into a system that over the course of centuries firmly established itself as a world religion.

It makes you wonder how some people can believe that such a world revolution that Christianity put into motion can come about from the exalted fiction of a few fanatics. It seems more realistic to presume the opposite: that what preceded Christianity in the ancient mystery religions served as a preparation for the very real events that occurred in the Holy Land two thousand years ago; that this event was looked for by those who knew, and longed for by those who only believed; that the coming of Christ was seen as the fulfilment of the old mystery schooling, and that what had previously been experienced only in the souls of individuals, namely the birth of the Son of God, had finally been made visible on the stage of the world.

This is how I would like to consider the events surrounding Jesus Christ in the subsequent chapters. But before we do so, it is worth going deeper into the mystery character of the gospels themselves.

3

Mystery Wisdom and the Gospels

The similarities between the gospel accounts and the teachings of the ancient mystery schools has already been referred to. But it is precisely this mystery character that has made the gospels harder to understand and easier to dismiss as time has gone on. In the eighteenth and nineteenth centuries, theologians, philologists and historians subjected the gospels to textual, historical and literary analysis, just as they would any other piece of literature or historical document. As a result, what had previously been intuitively felt to form a living whole was torn to pieces.

A divide developed between the so-called synoptic gospels of Matthew, Mark and Luke on the one hand, and John's gospel on the other. The latter was viewed as unhistorical, idealistic and philosophical, and was therefore dismissed as unreliable, even though John was an eyewitness (according to tradition Matthew was also a witness to events). By contrast, the three synoptic gospels, in spite of their mutual differences and a few painfully evident contradictions, were viewed as historically more reliable. The assumption was that they derived from the same oral tradition of eyewitnesses.

Because the mystery character of these texts was not properly understood, it was also no longer understood that each gospel throws light on just one aspect of the being of Jesus Christ, and that only the four different descriptions together form a more rounded picture, which nevertheless is still far from complete.

Especially in liberal Protestant circles there was a growing tendency towards a view of Christ that stripped him of all divinity, mystery and depth. He became the 'simple man from Nazareth', the gentle, compassionate carpenter's son, whose charitable intentions were not understood, and who was executed to prevent a popular revolution by a crowd that was stirred up by Jewish priests.

Conversely, in the estsablished churches around the world, emphasis is placed precisely on Christ's divinity as the Son of God. His deeds are considered miracles that need no further explanation, nor even admit of such. These more conservative Christians may think they are acknowledging the mystery character of Christianity, but what they call 'mystery' is in fact nothing but dogmas and rules laid down by Church councils over the millennia. They have nothing to do with a spiritual understanding of the gospels which, in their fourfoldness, reveal the secret of the divine as well as the human in Jesus Christ. The actual mystery character of the four gospels, which connects these scriptures with the pre-Christian paths of initiation, is disregarded by traditional Christianity, which has been opposed to it from the very beginning.

Thanks to the spiritual research of Rudolf Steiner, however, we have a wealth of new insights not only into the reality of Christ, but also into the origin and nature of the four canonical gospels. In numerous lectures Steiner discusses the specific aspect of each separate gospel, while also explaining the mutual relationships that exist between these scriptures. For now, I only want to highlight a few interesting points.

In his lectures on the Gospel of Luke, Steiner points out that a distinction must be made between clairvoyants and initiates if you want to understand sources from which the gospel writers drew. Broadly speaking there are three levels of higher consciousness that human beings can raise themselves to in order to know and experience the spiritual world: imagination, inspiration and intuition. Those who have developed imaginative cognition and possess the ability to behold spiritual images may be called clairvoyants. The Greek word used refer to such individuals in the gospels is *autoptai* (singular, *autoptes*), which is usually translated as 'eyewitnesses' (Lk 1:3). However, this does not mean people who saw events with their physical eyes, but people who with their own (*autos*) organs of spiritual perception could behold (*optai,* which is related to the verb 'to see') the events in a spiritual light without being physically present.

But although these 'beholders' did indeed see images of spiritual realities, they were not able to explain them. To grasp the deeper significance of what is seen in imagination, higher levels of consciousness are required, namely inspiration and intuition. In inspiration, spiritual sounds and words are perceived, we begin to hear the beings of the higher worlds speaking to us; in intuition we become one with the being of the other. This becoming one with the other through cognitive activity is also the highest form of love; on this level, love and cognition fully coincide. In the intuitive condition of consciousness, the I of the individual also remains fully intact. Those who have developed these higher spiritual capacities are called initiates. To them the lower and higher beings that populate the spiritual worlds reveal their inner nature through spiritual sounds and words.

These initiates have access to the secrets of the Word, and the author of the Gospel of John should be regarded as such an initiate. Luke considers himself a 'servant of the Word', not one of those whom you could call 'possessors of the Word'. He says that his gospel is based on the communications of 'self-seers' and 'servants of the Word'. In the rendering of the New Testament by Jon Madsen the Gospel of Luke begins as follows:

> Many have already set themselves the task of describing in the right sequence and stages the events which have been fulfilled among us. The tidings have been passed on to us from those who, from the very beginning, have become self-seers and servants of the Word. And so I, too, must write down in the right order what has shown itself to me, now that I have carefully and exactly trodden the steps of the path from its beginning. I do this for you, honoured Friend of God: By your own insight may you now win through to certainty in all that you have come to know through the teaching you have received. (Lk 1:1–4)

Clairvoyant authors become 'servants of the Word' because what they have come to know through seeing they write down according to the insights provided to them by an initiate, one who has risen to inspired states of consciousness and has access to the deeper significance of events. John, who had risen to inspirative and intuitive consciousness, could speak from a higher standpoint than the three other evangelists, but he had his limitations when it came to the imaginative element of pictorial description, in which Matthew and Luke excelled.

In addition to the difference between clairvoyants and initiates, we can also speak of distinct soul capacities of the human being based on ancient mystery practices. In the fourfoldness of the canonical gospels these different soul capacities can also be clearly recognised.

When people undertake esoteric development, at some point they experience a split in their consciousness.[1] This occurs shortly before and during the crossing of the threshold that separates ordinary day consciousness from suprasensory consciousness. The three functions of the soul, thinking, feeling and willing, which in normal circumstances work together in a certain harmony regulated by the I, separate out and begin to lead lives of their own as it were. Thoughts, feelings and impulses of will act without mutual cohesion and only the strengthened power of the I can maintain the balance in the diverging soul life. It is not an exaggeration when this division occurs to speak of these soul faculties as three separate beings within the individual: a thinking being, a feeling being and a being of will, each with their own specific traits.

In the ancient mysteries these traits were cultivated by means of initiation practices that deliberately developed the three soul functions in a one-sided manner. Thus there were mystery places where the wisdom element predominated in correlation with the human capacity to think. The initiates of these mysteries were the 'knowing ones' who bore the light of wisdom in themselves to the highest degree. In other places, feeling was developed in the most complete way. The love, devotion and readiness to sacrifice that the initiates acquired in such a mystery schooling made them healers and physicians. In ancient times healing was a feeling process that worked between patient and healer. A schooling of the will led to the development of magical capacities. The initiates of these mysteries were able to work out of their trained willpower to form and change even the materiality of things. Finally, there were also mysteries where the pupil strove for a certain harmony among the three soul faculties. You could call these the mysteries of humanness.

These four paths of schooling were represented by four symbols from the zodiac: the eagle (a substitute for Scorpio), Taurus the bull, Leo the lion, and Aquarius the water carrier, or human being. When you look at these signs in the circle of the zodiac you will see that the Eagle (or Scorpio as it currently is) stands opposite Taurus, and Leo stands opposite Aquarius. If you draw lines connecting these signs, the lines form a cross.

Intellectual thinking will view such a picture at best as a curious symbol from ancient times, but the mythological picture consciousness of ancient cultures that preceded abstract thinking saw in this cross of four animals a being: a mighty imagination of the primal cosmic image of the human being.[2]

Now, those who lived at the time of Christ's incarnation and who still had a connection to the ancient mystery culture, when they took Christ into their souls experienced in him the four capacities mentioned above. In Christ the four distinct mystery paths were not only united but made visible through the deeds he performed in the world.

It is understandable therefore that the life of Christ was also described in a fourfold way in the gospels, and that the four evangelists should be associated with the four zodiac signs mentioned above. The eagle, the animal of the thinking initiate John, whose gospel is the revelation of the highest wisdom. This revelation is summed up in the words of Christ: 'I am the Light of the world' (Jn 8:12). The bull, representing the Greek physician and seer Luke, whose gospel is the revelation of the highest sacrificial love. The bull was the preeminent sacrificial animal as depicted in the Egyptian and later Persian Mithras mysteries. You could summarise Luke's revelation of love and compassion with the words Christ speaks during his crucifixion: 'Father, forgive them for they know not what they do' (Lk 23:14). The lion, symbolising Mark in whose gospel the mighty lion nature of the Christ being is depicted along with the revelation of the highest magical willpower. Finally, there is the revelation of humanness in Matthew's gospel which, of the four, most emphasises Jesus as the son of David and represents Christ as a human being in all his aspects.

When you grasp the fittingness of the viewpoints mentioned here, you not only see the differences between the four gospels in a new light, but it becomes clear that one gospel is not more important or historically more accurate than another. They have been so composed that the picture given by each one places one specific aspect in the foreground, which in the other three remains more in the background or is not even mentioned at all.

What we must not lose sight of, however, is the fact that all four gospel stories agree on the same three things: Christ's baptism in the Jordan, his death on the cross, and his resurrection. In the following chapters I will give most of my attention to these three events, allowing for the opportunity to discuss the distinct aspects and profound differences of the four gospels.

But before we can approach the mystery of the baptism, we must first consider the figure of Jesus of Nazareth, and delve into the descriptions given by Matthew and Luke, who, right at the beginning of their gospels, show such remarkable differences.

4

Jesus of Nazareth

The events that took place two thousand years ago in the Holy Land can only be understood if we keep in mind the entire evolution of the world and humanity up to that time. In contrast to the current materialistic worldview, which sees human beings as having developed out of more primitive animals, Rudolf Steiner's spiritual science states that the history of humanity is not only a descent, but also a gradual decline from the spiritual heights out of which humanity and its successive cultures have sprung.

As human beings began to feel more at home on earth, taking hold of material existence and using it for their own benefit, they gradually lost their immediate awareness of the world of the spirit. They became so attached to matter that they experienced an inward darkening. Even the life after death was no longer experienced as a return to a realm of light where they were reunited with the gods and their ancestors. Instead, it was seen as an aimless, melancholy wandering through the dark, chilly realm of Hades. For the Greeks, underlying the delight they took in the beauty and vigour of physical life was a gloomy feeling that humanity was ultimately doomed to die. This tragic mood was summed up by Homer in his *Odyssey* when the ghost of Achilles says to Odysseus that he would rather 'slave on earth … than rule down here over all the breathless dead.'[1]

The true initiates, however, who could still see into the realm of the gods to some extent, knew that one day the divine spirit, who bore the fullness of the divine realm within himself, would appear on earth in human form to heal humanity and lead it upward again. Many ordinary people lived in the hope and expectation of this World Saviour too.

The initiates also knew that the coming of this divine saviour had been in preparation for a long time, and that when the predestined time came, a human being would be born who, in his outer and inner nature, would be able to serve as the vessel for the divine spirit. According to the Jewish prophets, this person would be born of the royal line of the Hebrew people and would bear the name of Jesus.

Two of the four evangelists speak of the forming of this human vessel into which the Christ spirit would be received, and yet they do so in thoroughly different ways. Around the figure of Jesus there is a secret that traditional Christianity has carefully concealed, but which the Gospel writers have pointed to with sufficient clarity. The incarnation of Christ was prepared for within two different streams that are connected to the whole development of humanity.

This not only comes to expression in the two very different birth stories found in Matthew and Luke, but also in the genealogies they each give. Matthew's genealogy begins with Abraham, the forefather of the Hebrew people, and descends through three times fourteen generations to Jesus (Mt 1:1–17). Luke's begins with Jesus and goes back in time: Jesus, the son of Joseph, the son of Heli, the son of Matthat… and so on. Luke, like Matthew, goes back to Abraham, but he then continues further back in time via the great figures of Shem, Noah, Lamech, Methuselah, and ending with 'Enosh, the son of Seth, the son of Adam, the son of God' (Lk 3:23–28).

Now, you might think that this difference in counting backwards or forwards in time is not so important, and that Luke only wanted to emphasise that Jesus came from God, so his genealogy is a bit longer than that of Matthew's. But if you read both genealogies carefully you will see that between Joseph and King David the names are different. In Matthew the line from David to Jesus descends via Solomon, the great king of Israel, whereas in Luke it goes via Nathan.

The names of Jesus's forefathers in between – twenty-five in Matthew and forty in Luke – are so different from each other that it is impossible that this could be due to mistakes. Two sets of names appear in both lists, Shealtiel and Zerubbabel, but nothing indicates that these refer to the same persons in the two genealogies, and several names occur more than once – the name Joseph appears in Luke's list three times, for example. Therefore, we may presume that the descendants of Solomon and Nathan were different people, even if on occasions they shared the same name.

Who was this Nathan mentioned in Luke?

He was not the wise man who so prominently rebuked King David (2Sm 12), but rather a son of David and Bathsheba about whom very little is known other than that he was a priestly figure.

This remarkable difference between the two genealogies of Jesus has not been satisfactorily explained by Bible critics. At the same time, they have ignored the most obvious explanation, which is that it indicates two lines of descent from King David: a royal one through his son Solomon, and a priestly one through his other son Nathan. In their accounts of the nativity, Matthew and Luke are describing the births of two different Jesus children to two different sets of parents.

As mentioned in the previous chapter, the Dead Sea Scrolls found near the Essene settlement in Qumran, speak of the expectation of two Messiah figures, a priestly one 'from Aaron' and a royal one 'from Israel'. Since the 'Nathan' Jesus child described by Luke has no blood relationship to the tribe of Levi (Aaron was a priest of Levi), I presume that the indication 'from Aaron' refers to a spiritual origin, not a physical one. The words 'from Israel' then mean the specifically royal line of descent, with which the physical line is in agreement. In other apocryphal scriptures and in *The Sohar*, the classical book of the Jewish mystical doctrine known as the Kabbalah, allusions can also be found to the secret of the double Jesus figure.

As a result of his ability to read the Akashic Record, Rudolf Steiner not only confirmed the birth of two Jesus children and the two lines of descent from King David, but he also added details that the gospels do not mention. Many people may find this shocking and so it is worth placing these details in a greater context, which hopefully will make them more acceptable. What follows, therefore, is an account of the mystery of Jesus as drawn largely from the spiritual research of Rudolf Steiner, which he carried out through a precise and rigorously schooled spiritual consciousness.

The 'Solomon' Jesus child, whose birth is described by Matthew, was the legal king of Judea, having descended from the original royalty of Israel. His 'star', meaning his spiritual individuality, was beheld by three wise seers, who are often called kings or magi, the latter term referring to members of the Zoroastrian priesthood, the ancient Persian religion founded by the great initiate Zarathustra. Two of the kings came from Sheba, in modern-day Yemen, and the third from Ethiopia. They first went to Jerusalem and enquired of Herod, the reigning king of Judea, where they might find this person whose star they beheld and whom they knew to be the 'King of the Jews'.[2] Herod's chief priests, following the indications of the Jewish prophets, directed them to Bethlehem where they found the royal child and offered him their gifts of gold, frankincense and myrrh. The parents of this child, both of whom descended from the tribe of Judah, the same tribe as King David, lived in Bethlehem. That child was not born in a stable but in a house.

Herod, meanwhile, was concerned. He was from a non-Jewish family from Edom (south-western Jordan and the Negev today) and was merely a figurehead of the Roman rulers. He was afraid that if this child reached adulthood and claimed his royal position, he would lose his throne. He therefore ordered that all boys in Bethlehem and its surroundings who were two years old and under should be killed. However, Jesus's father, Joseph, was warned in a dream and escaped with Mary and the child into Egypt where they stayed in Heliopolis.[3]

After Herod's death they returned to the Holy Land, but instead of Bethlehem they settled in Nazareth in faraway Galilee. Due to their two-year absence, they had not only escaped the attention of Herod, but also that of the Jewish priests, whose Messianic expectations had been directed towards these parents. Jesus grew up in Nazareth with brothers and sisters who were born after him.

In Nazareth there lived another family, also from the tribe of Judah but not descended from the royal line of David. Joseph, a carpenter, his young wife, Mary, and their little son, who was also called Jesus. This is the family mentioned in Luke.

Luke describes how one day, Joseph and Mary had to travel to Bethlehem from Nazareth for a census ordered by the Emperor Augustus. Mary was pregnant and gave birth to her baby in a stable in Bethlehem where they had finally found shelter in the crowded little town. Shepherds in the fields outside the town were told by a heavenly voice that the long-expected Messiah had been born. They went and found the child in the stable and offered him their humble gifts. This is the nativity story we are most familiar with, although nothing is mentioned in Luke's gospel about a visit by kings. The child was circumcised according to the Jewish rite and presented in the temple according to Jewish law, where the wise seer Simeon and the old prophetess Anna gave their blessings and Simeon gave his prophetic warning to Mary about her son's destiny (Lk 2:29–31, 36). The parents returned to Nazareth with their baby where, after some time, they met the other 'holy family' and befriended them.

We might wonder if the birth of this Jesus child from the Nathan line of David's dynasty only takes place after Herod has died, or whether there are other reasons why this descendant received so little attention. After all the commotion of the arrival of the three wise men from the East, and after the failed attempt by Herod to find and kill the child in Bethlehem, things in Judea had quietened down to some extent. The unknown family from Nazareth, which, despite the rumours spread among the people by the shepherds in

Bethlehem at the time of their son's birth, had not drawn the attention of the priests in Jerusalem, remained undisturbed.

Nazareth at the time was a settlement of the Essenes, and these two children grew up among these pious people, who may have had some insight into the secret of the two children.

While the evangelists say little about these two children, several beautiful legends give descriptions of them and their very different natures, although they are never both mentioned in the same story. The royal Solomon Jesus was incredibly wise and alert. In everything he said and did he showed the maturity of someone who has gone through many incarnations and gained remarkable wisdom. The Nathan Jesus on the other hand showed no particular aptitude for anything. He had a dreamy nature and a kind of angelic purity and was filled with love and compassion for the people around him. He was not of this world and moved everyone with his heavenly innocence and naiveté. The two children grew up not far from each other and, despite their contrasting natures, became close friends.

Some years later, a remarkable event took place that is only recorded by Luke. At the end of the second chapter of his gospel he relates how the family went to Jerusalem every year to celebrate Passover. When the Nathan Jesus was twelve years old, they made the trip as usual, but on their way back Mary and Joseph realised their son was no longer with them. Filled with worry, they returned to Jerusalem to look for him. After three days they found him in the temple, explaining the scriptures to an audience of astonished and learned rabbis like an accomplished scholar. Mary and Joseph rebuked him and asked him why he would cause them such anxiety. Jesus replied: 'Why did you look for me? Do you not know that

I must be in my Father's house?', but his parents 'did not understand what he said to them' (Lk 2:49f).

Behind this event something very important must lie hidden, otherwise the evangelist would not have made a point of recording it. Spiritual research reveals that during the three days the Nathan child could not be found, the I or individuality of the Solomon Jesus, who had also come to Jerusalem for the Passover festival with his parents, moved into the soul and body of this boy. The two children became one in an intimate, inward process that was hidden from outer eyes, but which nevertheless manifested in outward behaviour. This is the reason why the 'simple' Nathan child could suddenly speak like a teacher, where before he had shown no real scholarly talents. From that moment on, the mature individuality of the royal child filled the descendant from the priestly line.

According to Rudolf Steiner, the Solomon boy died shortly after this event. Without the sustaining power of his I he could not live much longer.

There is now one Jesus figure standing before us, in whom two streams of humanity have been united. We will see what is meant by this when we penetrate more deeply into the spiritual reality that underpins the outer event.

In many cultures throughout the world we find traditions concerning a blissful, primeval time in humanity when illness, old age and death did not yet exist, and human beings lived in close connection with the divine powers that had created them. But this time came to an end through the intervention of less exalted spiritual beings who rebelled against the good powers and tore human beings away from the divine world of their origin.

Rudolf Steiner's research confirms these mythological traditions and gives extensive descriptions of the above-mentioned intervention by what he calls Luciferic spirits – spirits of pride and egotism.[4] In the Old Testament this is known as the Fall.

Since that time the decline indicated at the beginning of this chapter has set in, and this has had profound consequences for the development of humanity. For while this decline has meant that earthly humanity has been liberated in a sense from being embedded in higher worlds – we have acquired a certain autonomy in our consciousness – this has come at an alarmingly high cost.

Human beings can stray from God in two ways. They can stray in the realm of morality by following egotistic inclinations and desires, in which case they fall prey to Lucifer. But they can also stray in the realm of insight and understanding by harbouring bad or incorrect thoughts and exercising poor judgment. They then come under the influence of Ahriman or Satan, the spirit of lies who wants to chain human beings to matter.[5]

In Genesis we find this duality pictured in the two trees of Paradise: the Tree of Life and the Tree of the Knowledge of Good and Evil. When Adam and Eve ate from the Tree of the Knowledge of Good and Evil, they were cast out of Paradise and condemned to die. Death is a consequence of our knowledge-filled consciousness.

In the long development of humanity we can therefore distinguish two streams that correspond with the two trees of Paradise: a stream of knowledge or wisdom and a stream of life and love. The stream of knowledge could also be called the royal stream. Kings wear golden crowns with precious stones set in them. This is the sign of wisdom: precious stones represent the stars and gold indicates the sun, for originally the stream of knowledge was fed from cosmic sources of wisdom, and the Tree of Knowledge still had much heavenly life in it. Only later, when knowledge became intellectualistic, did this tree die.

The stream of life and love could be called the shepherds' stream or the priestly stream. A shepherd or priest watches over his flock not through heavenly knowledge, but through his sympathy and love, which are of the earth. It is only on earth that human beings develop compassion for their fellow creatures and seek to protect them from evil. These two streams can be clearly observed in the succession of earthly cultures, where they sometimes work in combination, for example in the priest-kings of several peoples.

The leading figures of these two streams had to protect the purity of knowledge and moral chastity of the human being. The 'true King' had to fight against lies, untruth, and bad thoughts; the 'true Shepherd' had to watch over moral purity and protect his flock from the 'wolf' of desire and other temptations.

One day, however, death must be vanquished. In other words, the consequences of the Fall or separation from the divine realm must be reversed. One day, human beings must, in full freedom, bring about their reunification with God. The two trees of Paradise must be joined. The working of the spiritual beings who caused the falling away from God, and whose influence has over the course of time become stronger, must be brought to an end. If this did not happen, human beings would not be able to continue their development on earth in a positive sense; they would become entangled in evil.

The consequences of that are shown to us in the last book in the Bible, the Apocalypse of John.

For this to be accomplished, however, a high divine being would need to connect himself with humanity and the earth. This being, acknowledged as the highest god in the ancient mysteries, had to find a human vehicle in which the union of the most developed representative of the wisdom stream with the most perfect representative of the stream of love and life had come about.

The individuality who incarnated in the Solomon Jesus child, and whose star was beheld by the wise kings who worshipped this individuality as their spiritual leader, was none other than Zarathustra, the great initiate of the ancient Persian cultural epoch.

Zarathustra was the son of a Persian king, and he founded Zoroastrianism, his sun religion, many thousands of years before Christ. At that time, he beheld the highest god in the spiritual sphere of the sun. Known as Ahura Mazdao, the Great Aura, this was the mighty divine being who would one day descend to earth and overcome the destructive power of the spirit of lies, Angra Mainyu, or Ahriman as he was later called.

Zarathustra incarnated many times, dedicating himself in each incarnation to helping prepare for the coming of the sun spirit on earth. In the sixth century BC, he lived in Babylon during the Babylonian exile of the Jewish people and was called Nazarathos or Zarathas.[6] He was the initiated teacher of the Jewish prophets Ezekiel and Daniel, and also of the Greek philosopher Pythagoras.[7] In the Avesta, the holy book of the Persians, we find an unmistakable reference to a future incarnation of Zarathustra as the saviour into whom the sun spirit will descend. Alongside the prophets of the Old Testament, it is probably one of the most tremendous prophecies of Christ from pre-Christian ages:

> The mighty, the kingly Sun-Ether-Aura bearing
> prophecy,
> The divinely created one,
> We venerate in prayer,
> Which will pass over the most victorious of the
> saviours,
> And to the other, his Apostles,
> Which will bring the world forward,
> Allowing the world to overcome age and death,
> Decay and decline,
> Which helps the world to eternal life,
> To eternal prosperity,
> To free will,
> When the dead will rise again,
> When the last conqueror of death comes
> And through the will the world will be brought
> forward.
> (Yasht 19, 89)[8]

Thus, from the child whose birth is described in Matthew there spoke the individuality of one of humanity's greatest initiates. For centuries he had helped prepare the people who would one day create the vessel for the divine spirit, and among whom he would appear in his incarnation as Jesus. He accomplished this preparation not only as the teacher of the great prophets in Babylon, but earlier, through one of his most important students who had incarnated as Moses.[9] Moses gave to his people the Law, the purpose of which was to preserve the connection to the divine spirit down through the generations via blood relationships and inherited capacities. Then, through the person of Jesus, the spirit would take the place of the Law through the free, moral, creative power of love.

But the individuality of the royal Jesus had first to unite with the stream of life and love represented by the other Jesus from the Nathan line of King David's descendants.

This Nathan child was not a human being in the usual sense. The great Church Father Origen considered this Jesus to be the paradisal soul of the first human being, the *anima candida,* the pure soul, who was not part of the Fall.[10] He agreed with the Jewish mystical tradition that speaks of the light of the higher soul that fled from Adam when he was driven out of Paradise. This higher part of the soul of Adam, which was of an angelic nature, remained in the sphere of the Tree of Life, where the higher spiritual powers and beings can be found who do not clothe themselves in material existence. From there, this pure soul was able to unfold spiritual activities of great significance for the rest of humanity on earth.[11]

In order to become the saviour of humanity, the Nathan soul had to incarnate on earth for the first time. He did not have a 'normal' human I, one that had been formed through many earthly incarnations; he had not incurred guilt due to sin and therefore possessed no karma. But he did possess the full freshness of the Tree of Life: he was pure compassion and sacrificial love.

The Nathan child was also the representative of the stream of life and love in another respect. In his astral body (the soul) there worked the spiritual power of the greatest teacher of love and compassion who, in his last incarnation in India, had been the Buddha. From spiritual heights, his soul being, or nirmanakaya, shone into the Jesus child.[12] This radiance was perceived by the shepherds in the fields near Bethlehem as an angel accompanied by the heavenly host, praising God and sending a message of peace to all people of good will.

Many aspects of the secret concerning Jesus of Nazareth have not been touched upon in this chapter. I will continue these contemplations in the next chapter, drawing in particular on the lecture cycle Rudolf Steiner gave called *The Fifth Gospel.*[13] These contain descriptions of the eighteen years during which the I of Zarathustra lived and worked in the physical and soul sheaths of the Nathan Jesus, until it withdrew to make way for the Christ spirit at the baptism in the Jordan. Neither the canonical nor the apocryphal gospels contain any reports of these years. The great forerunner to Jesus Christ, John the Baptist, and the two Marys will also be discussed.

5

The Fifth Gospel

Before returning to the story of Jesus of Nazareth, we must pause to consider the women who brought the two totally different Jesus children into the world. Here, too, we find a secret concerning two individuals who, in a sense, had the same double origin as their firstborn children and who at a certain moment also became one.

Both the mothers in their earthly appearance were a reflection of the heavenly woman mentioned in gnostic writings as the goddess Sophia.[1] Both 'Marys' were connected with the paradisal primeval beginning of humanity. Like the Nathan Jesus, the mother of this child was herself a heavenly being who incarnated on earth for a short time to bear the heavenly child, and to show humanity once again the earthly appearance of the Eternal Feminine. Everything that later painters, especially Raphael,[2] have tried to represent in their Madonnas – the purest loveliness and feminine beauty together with the highest worthiness – is present in this virgin mother bestowing life and blessing.

Nothing is known about where the mother of the Nathan Jesus came from, and only the initiated Essenes of Nazareth may have known who she was. She had been given to Joseph, the simple carpenter, as his wife. Medieval painters sometimes pictured her in a garden, and that is how we should also imagine her, surrounded by blossoming plants and playful animals: the dreaming soul in Paradise.

The archangel Gabriel appeared to her and announced the birth of the Messiah. It is clear that the higher beings already viewed this child as being connected with Christ: 'He will be great, he will be called the Son of the Highest God' (Lk 1:32). Mary replied: 'How will this be, since I have never known a man?' She was not conscious of the fertilisation that by then had taken place. This is the reason for her immaculateness, namely a conception that took place during sleep without desire. Joseph likewise had no awareness concerning this.

In the early stages of humanity, human reproduction was more a concern of the gods than human beings, who remained unconscious during the process. This is indicated in Genesis when God causes Adam to fall into a deep sleep before creating Eve from one of Adam's ribs (Gn 2:21). This primordial condition was eventually replaced by the conscious, desire-driven joining of the two sexes that we know today. But the divine guidance that prepared the coming of Christ, kept the mother and father of the Nathan Jesus in that earlier, supra-personal, consecrated state, which is what is meant by Jesus being conceived by the Holy Spirit.

Six months before the announcement to Mary in Galilee, another remarkable event had occurred in Judea which many today might consider an implausible miracle. However, it becomes understandable if you take into account that in earlier times people were different in their psychic and physical nature than we are today. Mary's cousin, the aged Elizabeth, had become pregnant. She had married the priest Zechariah a long time ago, but the couple had remained childless. Now Elizabeth was suddenly expecting.

During his service in the temple, Zechariah had been visited by the archangel Gabriel who told him that his wife would bear a son whom he was to call John: 'He will be great in the sight of the Lord ... bearing within him the spirit and the power of Elijah' (Lk 1:15–17). Zechariah refused to believe the angel and was struck dumb as a result, only regaining his speech when his son was born.

The contrast in the composition is not only striking but full of significance. In the barren country of Judea an old woman becomes pregnant; the announcement is made to the old man. In Nazareth, in the fertile, blooming region of Galilee, the announcement comes to the very young girl who, unconsciously, will conceive from the spirit.

The child expected by Elizabeth was an old soul, the oldest of humanity: Adam. Of him Christ later said: 'among all those who are born of women there is none who is greater than John' (Lk 7:28). Mary, by contrast, would bear the youngest child of humanity: the new Adam, who had preserved the heavenly soul in the heights of heaven until such time as he could incarnate to fulfil his sacrificial deed on earth.

The encounter between Mary and Elizabeth, known as the Visitation, during which Elizabeth feels John leaping in her womb (Lk 1:41), is not simply a moving family scene, rather it points to a profound meaning. It reveals the intimate connection that exists between the souls of these two unborn children who, as it were, share a single I, and which is awakened in John by the encounter.

In this Mary of Luke's gospel, the soul of Eve is re-embodied. This is something that people have sensed through the centuries. In the hymn 'Ave Maria' there sounds the reverse of Eva, and although 'Ave' (be greeted!) was a commonly used word in Latin, people in the Middle Ages still experienced this reversal in it.

On the other hand, the mother of the Solomon Jesus was known to the Jewish priests and scribes. Her birth and childhood are described in an apocryphal gospel that offered medieval and renaissance artists rich material for their frescoes and sculptures. Just like John the Baptist, Mary was born from aged parents, Joachim and Hanna. She was accepted into the service of the temple in Jerusalem, where among the young girls she was an example of devotion, wisdom and purity. She was quick to learn and hardworking.

When she reached the marriageable age of fourteen and was no longer able to serve as a temple maiden, she was given to Joseph as his bride. This Joseph was a descendant of King David who had reigned over the whole area of the twelve tribes of Israel. Mary wanted to remain in the temple and did not wish to marry, but obeying a directive from the divine world the priests summoned all unmarried men, young and old, from the tribe of Judah to Jerusalem. They were told to bring the twig of a tree. Joseph, who was much older than Mary, came with an unsightly little twig because he assumed there was no chance that he would ever marry this young beautiful girl. However, it was through this little twig, overlooked at first because of its size, that the divine sign was revealed: the twig suddenly bloomed and a white dove flew out of it when the priest took it from the altar. Mary accepted the divine decision and moved with Joseph to his home in Bethlehem.

Then Mary became pregnant before she had been with Joseph. Not wanting to put her to shame, Joseph considered divorcing Mary quietly, but in a dream the angel of the Lord revealed to him that Mary had conceived by the Holy Spirit and he did not need to reject her. Joseph was told that Mary would bear a son whom they should call Jesus, and who would save his people from their sins (Mt 1:18–25).

Here, too, the 'miracle' of the immaculate conception took place, but in a somewhat different way than for the couple in Nazareth. The Mary and Joseph in Matthew's gospel conceived their child in a temple sleep that was brought about by the priests.[3] At the time, this consecrated temple sleep was no longer practiced, but an exception was made by the priests of the temple for the parents of the Solomon Jesus because they expected that the Messiah would be born to them. Because we no longer know anything about these ancient mystery customs, it has led people to interpret the concept of the virgin birth physically, as if it means there had been no union between Mary and Joseph. However, 'virginal' in this context means that conception took place in an unconscious, supra-personal state, just as it had in primeval times. The offspring who were thus begotten in this 'paradisal' way, without the personal desire of the parents, was considered to be conceived by the Holy Spirit. For both the mother and child this meant 'immaculateness', the purity of the astral body was preserved.

We can now return to the story of the two Jesus children and the moment the I of the Solomon or Zarathustra Jesus passed over into the body of the Nathan Jesus child. The Solomon Jesus, having sacrificed his I, died soon after the return of both families to Nazareth. There were those in Israel for whom the Solomon Jesus was the focus of their Messianic expectations, and it is interesting to note that in certain Jewish circles still today the conviction exists that the Messiah was indeed born at that time, but that he died young. The mystery of the two Jesus figures becoming one escaped the Jewish initiates, except perhaps the Essenes. Orthodox Jewish doctrine could not, and still cannot, accept that a different Jesus, not of royal descent, may have been the bearer of the Messiah.

When the two Jesus children became one, the I of the Zarathustra individuality lived on in the pure sheaths of the paradisal, heavenly Nathan Jesus child. Luke says of him: 'And Jesus progressed in wisdom, in maturity and in grace in the sight of God and men' (Lk 2:52). This translation by Jon Madsen follows the remarks Rudolf Steiner made about this passage. The New International Version has: 'And Jesus grew in wisdom and stature, and in favour with God and man.'

But what would be the sense in reporting something obvious, namely that a growing child would increase in stature or years? In Greek, the language in which Luke wrote his gospel, it says that Jesus increased *en tē sophia kai ēlikia, kai chariti.* With the three words *sophia, ēlikia* and *chariti* Luke wanted to indicate that Jesus developed in a threefold manner to prepare for his future sacrificial deed of receiving the Christ being. He increased in wisdom (*sophia*), because his soul or astral body was ennobled and irradiated by the wise I of Zarathustra. But this also penetrated into his life body or etheric body (*ēlikia*), meaning that his habits and inclinations matured by the wisdom of his soul. Finally, his physical form and facial features developed a graceful beauty (*chariti*).

Soon after the death of the Solomon Jesus, the Nathan Mary also died. Her husband, Joseph, the carpenter, married the other Mary, the mother of the Solomon Jesus, whose husband had died some time before. The two holy families had now also become one. The Nathan Jesus grew up with brothers and sisters with whom he had no blood relationship, although he was connected to them through the Zarathustra I that now lived in him. In the years that followed, however, no strong connection with this family developed, except with his stepmother, the Solomon Mary.

In 1913, in his lecture cycle *The Fifth Gospel,* Rudolf Steiner described pictures from the Akashic Record of Jesus's life between the ages of twelve and thirty, before the Christ descended into him at the baptism in the Jordan.[4] The tone of these lectures is extremely intimate, and the reader can sense that behind his descriptions a profound emotion is stirring. Indeed, Steiner explained to his audience that it was a great effort for him to speak about what he had beheld. A concise account like the present one can hardly be expected to have the same effect, and for that reason I would recommend that the reader read the original lecture cycle. It is my intention here to present a simple summary of the spiritual viewpoints that throw new light on the being and work of Christ and his bearer, Jesus of Nazareth.

The unknown eighteen years of Jesus's life – from the scene in the temple in Jerusalem when he was twelve years old to the baptism in the Jordan – can be divided into three periods of six years. During this time he travelled the region doing the simple manual work of his father. Until his twelfth year, Jesus had lived in innocence about the world; human suffering and the power of evil were unknown to him. Now he had to learn to know this power through his encounters with the people he met. He shared intensely in their sufferings and their feelings of being forsaken by God, and he experienced how far they had strayed from the divine world in all their hubris and egotism.

According to Steiner, Jesus of Nazareth had his first experience of this kind among the representatives of his own people, the scribes and the Pharisees. The event in the temple in Jerusalem had brought about a radical transformation in him: from the formerly dreamy child he had suddenly become an earnest young thinker who immersed himself in the scriptures, visited the synagogues, and had discussions with rabbis and priests. He drew inspiration from the spirit of the Hebrew people and the stream of divine revelation that had worked down through the ages in the patriarchs, the prophets, and the first kings of Israel. The awakened I of Zarathustra grew ever more strongly within him.

But it soon became clear that what inspired and enlightened him, the spirit that had moved the old prophets, no longer worked in those who claimed to be the spiritual leaders of the chosen people. The voice of this spirit was silent for them, because through their cold intellectuality and arrogant orthodoxy they had closed themselves off to it. And even if this voice had still sounded, there were no longer any ears able to hear it. This caused Jesus terrible suffering, but he found he could not speak about this with anyone, not his father or stepmother, and certainly not his stepbrothers and stepsisters, who thought he was strange and often ridiculed him. He was extremely lonely.

In the second period of six years, Jesus came into contact with the pagan world. He travelled a lot with his work, leading an almost itinerant lifestyle as he visited different places in the wider region. He met a great many people and according to Steiner his noble and loving character had a beneficial effect on them. The intense suffering he had experienced inwardly as a result of the God-forsakenness of his people had become transmuted into love. The compassion that he had borne within him from early childhood was so strong that he emanated a remarkable influence on those around him. When in the evening he sat with people and talked with them, they sensed this loving radiance, and when he had left again to work somewhere else, people continued to experience this effect as though he were still with them.

In his professional wanderings, Jesus also came across sacred places where pagan priests had once sought to bring people into contact with the spiritual powers that protected them. Here, too, he experienced, albeit in a different way than he had among his own people, how the spiritual stream of revelation that had been powerfully present in ancient times had all but dried up. The effect of this decline had led to demonic possession, illness and demoralisation among the surrounding people.

Rudolf Steiner describes how Jesus's awareness of this darkening decline among the pagan population reached its climax in an out-of-body experience he had in which he beheld the profoundly miserable situation of these people. This happened at the altar of one of the sacred places, which had been deserted by the priests who had fled because of the leprosy that was rife in the area.

When Jesus approached the place and the people saw him, they streamed to the altar, thinking that this person who radiated love and goodness, had come to renew the sacrificial service and reconcile them with the gods. This was not Jesus's intention at all, but the people crowded around him and lifted him onto the altar. In that moment he beheld in a mighty vision how at one time the forces of high divine beings had streamed down onto the holy places of sacrifice. But now, demons of all kinds crowded together on the altars, including Luciferic and Ahrimanic beings who caused illness and possession. Jesus experienced in mighty, supersensory images, the decline and fall of pagan culture. He fell down as though dead, and the terrified people ran away.

In this out-of-body condition, Jesus's spirit penetrated into the heights from which the original revelations of the pagan mystery religions had flowed. And just as he had experienced the prophetic spirit of the Hebrew people in himself as an inspiring voice that his Jewish contemporaries could no longer hear, now he heard mystery words concerning the secrets of human development that had been revealed to pagan initiates in primeval times. Steiner rendered these words in the form of a prayer that he called the macrocosmic Our Father:

> Amen.
> The evils hold sway,
> Witness of egoity releasing itself.
> Selfhood guilt through others incurred,
> Experienced in the daily bread,
> Wherein the will of the heavens does not rule,
> Because man separated himself from your realm,
> And forgot your names,
> You Fathers in the heavens.[5]

The Christ spirit, working through Jesus, would later reverse the sequence and the meaning of each petition. Whereas the macrocosmic Our Father expresses the decline and separation of humanity from its heavenly origin, the

Christian Lord's Prayer, as taught by Christ to his disciples, is a prayer of ascent. It describes the reconnection of human beings with the powers of heaven.

Jesus's experience at the pagan altar made him aware of the tragedy of pagan humanity, just as he had come to realise something similar in the case of the Jewish people. The more he was permeated by what had been revealed to him from the divine world, the more he felt the desolation of those who no longer shared in that world. This was the second source of his infinite sorrow for fellow human beings, which he also had to bear in loneliness.

When Jesus was about twenty-four, his father died. As the eldest son, he had to take on the responsibility of caring for the family. From then on he remained in the vicinity of Nazareth, living at home with his stepbrothers and -sisters and with his stepmother.

It was during this period in his life that Jesus came into closer contact with the Essene community in Nazareth.

As has already been mentioned, the Essenes lived an incredibly strict and ascetic way of life in order that they might, through inner purification, restore their connection to God. Their exercises consisted in a spiritual ascent along the path by which the Hebrew people had descended from Abraham over the centuries. They felt that they had to accomplish this path of initiation to prepare for the coming of the Messiah.

Jesus became a kind of lay member of their community, which meant he did not officially join the order, nor did he take part in their rites and exercises. Nevertheless, the members of the order recognised in him an initiated master and had no problem discussing with him their otherwise secret mystery teachings.

Jesus also met his cousin, John, the son of Elizabeth, at the Essene community. Like Jesus, John had developed a close relationship with the order without really becoming a member. Although John would soon feel the mighty call of destiny, there was no indication yet of Jesus's destiny – not for himself nor for the people around him. He was still absorbed by the suffering of humanity and the inner experiences of compassion and loneliness.

In his contacts with these Righteous Ones, however, Jesus noticed something that again filled him with terrible suffering. In the Essenes he had found people who, by way of devotion to the Law and through their pure way of life, had managed to restore their connection to the heavenly world. There were still people who knew how to lead a life of holiness. But what made Jesus uneasy about this was that the members of the order kept this holy life at a distance from the rest of the people. That did not sit well with the love and compassion that Jesus had for all people. He saw that this small community could indeed connect itself to the divine, but only at the expense of the rest of humanity, which had to toil away in daily existence chained to matter. Jesus realised that the spiritual striving of the Essenes was based on exclusivity.

This was brought home to him by an experience that made a deep impression on him. One day as Jesus was leaving the settlement, he saw two figures fleeing from the entrance gate. They were the spiritual powers he had come to know were stalking humanity: Ahriman, the spirit of lies who had looked out at him from the hardened intellectualism of the Jewish scribes, and Lucifer, the tempter and originator of all the evil to which pagan humanity had fallen victim. Jesus realised that precisely because they were turned back at the gate of the Righteous Ones, the Essenes, these two spirits raged all the more powerfully among the rest of humanity. By raising themselves up, the Essenes thrust others down more deeply into ruin.

Jesus could no longer rejoice in the Essene's way of life and the spiritual advancement they were able to achieve. His compassion lay with the rest of humanity who were being pushed down so that a small, select group could rise. Jesus now began to see Lucifer and Ahriman at the gates of other Essene settlements in the area. It was the third, deeply troubling experience that Jesus had at the way humanity had become lost in a hopeless decline, and which filled him with an even greater suffering.

It was not long after this, we are told by Steiner, that Jesus had a conversation with his stepmother that was of decisive significance. As has already been mentioned, Jesus had grown close to his stepmother, and found in her an understanding for the things that occupied him so intensely. In this conversation it was possible for Jesus to speak about what he had experienced these last eighteen years, his great compassion for the misery and God-forsakenness of people, and his pain at the hopelessness of the situation. He spoke about his threefold suffering caused by his encounters with Judaism, paganism, and the Essenes, about the decline of humanity from its cosmic connection in ancient times to its current loss and alienation from the spirit. He described his own lonely struggles and despair as he came to the realisation that the decline had reached its nadir and that all developmental impulses had died. Only a completely new macrocosmic power of rejuvenation and recreation would be able to revive progress for a positive future.

Rudolf Steiner said that the scene of this conversation in the Akashic Record belongs to the most moving spiritual impressions one can have, and that nothing else like it can be found anywhere in the total development of humanity.

The words that Jesus spoke carried a profound power to them, as if every word was alive and had wings that carried them from his heart to that of his stepmother. Not only his own suffering, but the whole meaning of human development streamed out of him and permeated the being of Mary. With every word his I flowed out of him as the I of the great initiate Zarathustra left the body in which it had lived and worked for eighteen years.

Running concurrently with this process, a kind of counter movement took place involving Jesus's stepmother. The spirit of the Nathan Mary, who had died some years previously, now penetrated from super-earthly spheres into the Solomon Mary. We should not imagine this permeation as a sudden event, but as a rather gradual occurrence. It happened in such a way that when Christ descended into Jesus at the baptism in the Jordan the Solomon Mary became virginal again.

In order to comprehend this mystery, we must overcome every prejudice of a material nature and of an ecclesiastically dogmatic one concerning the Virgin Mary.

The idea that permeation with a 'heavenly element', in this case a spiritual being of a high order, can bring about a restoration of virginity in the female organism, is not implausible when we remember how much physiological processes are dependent on psychic-spiritual forces. The fact that this could come about was because, during the conversation, Jesus's stepmother completely shared her stepson's pain and sorrow for humanity's suffering, which had transformed itself into love for all human beings. This had created such a strong bond between mother and son that the descent of Christ into the son also had a rejuvenating influence on the mother.

Jesus of Nazareth left his mother after the conversation in which his I streamed out of him with his words. As if in a dream – though not really dreaming but rather guided by a higher consciousness – he went on his way, directed by a higher will, to the place where John was baptising people in the waters of the river Jordan.

6

The Baptism

The Gospel of Mark opens with the following words:

> The beginning of the good news about Jesus the Messiah, the Son of God, as it is written in Isaiah the prophet:
>
> I will send my messenger ahead of you,
> who will prepare your way
> a voice of one calling in the wilderness,
> 'Prepare the way for the Lord,
> make straight paths for him.'
>
> And so John the Baptist appeared in the wilderness, preaching a baptism of repentance for the forgiveness of sins. The whole Judean countryside and all the people of Jerusalem went out to him. Confessing their sins, they were baptised by him in the River Jordan. John wore clothing made of camel's hair, with a leather belt round his waist, and he ate locusts and wild honey. (Mk 1:1–6 NIV)

In the previous chapter it was said that in John, the son of Elizabeth, there lived the individuality of Adam from Genesis. With this in mind, we should consider the enigmatic figure of the Baptist more closely and the central role he played in the descent of the Christ into Jesus of Nazareth.

Through John there worked a being from the higher hierarchies of the angels; it permeated him and made it possible for him to lead people to Christ. Early Christian icons and reliefs depicted the figure of the Baptist with angel's wings, often appearing as a gigantic figure next to the much smaller figure of Jesus. John was indeed 'the greatest of all those born of women' (Mt 11:11), which the old painters and sculptors wanted to make clear.

Rudolf Steiner also confirmed what is expressed in the gospel texts: namely, that in John the prophet Elijah was born again (Mt 17:12–13; Mk 9:13). Elijah was also a higher being who made use of a human being to go about among the people. When John began to preach, people experienced a similar effect as that of Elijah.

John the Baptist stood at the turning point of time. He was the last great prophet of a people that had been guided by prophecy for two thousand years, and at the same time the first herald of the spirit of humanity: through the power of his preaching and baptism he prepared the people to receive the coming Messiah. As we have seen, the inner constitution of a great many people at that time had become so barren that they were hardly able to take in spiritual impulses. Their connection to the spirit was so weak that a kind of soul death threatened them with spiritual paralysis. A tremendous world force was therefore needed to bring about a profound change in the consciousness of people, and this world force spoke through John. He is often portrayed as a voice crying out in the wilderness for people to repent, but the word usually translated as 'repent', *metanoia,* expresses much more than repentance. What John was calling for was a profound change in a person's state of mind, and to help people achieve this he performed his baptisms in the Jordan. People came in their hundreds, from the cities, the countryside, and from faraway places. The news that a great prophet had arisen in Israel had spread abroad; with his flaming words John had ignited sparks in cold hearts.

John's baptism, however, was not the simple sprinkling of water on the head like we see in baptismal ceremonies today. Rather, the person was submerged until a kind of near-death experience was induced.

According to Rudolf Steiner, at the moment of death the bearer of life forces in us, which he called the etheric body, separates from the physical body. Because the etheric body also provides the foundation of memory, when this separation occurs the human being sees their whole life unfurl before them in a mighty panorama of images, which they perceive in an instant. This is the origin of the saying that your life flashes before you just before you die.

Through his baptism, John was able to loosen the etheric body in the people who came to him and give them this experience. But what was the significance of this for the people he baptised? When the Bible speaks of the 'liberation' or 'forgiveness' of sins (the Greek word *aphesis* carries both meanings) achieved through the baptism by John, what it refers to is this process whereby human beings were detached from what shackled them to 'sin', to material existence, enabling them to behold the tableau of their life. The life review brought with it the realisation that a spiritual reality underpins and transcends material existence. For many people of that time who were firmly chained to material things, whether through power and wealth or through acute hardship, this near-death experience opened them to the divine spirit. In some cases, people were able to discern how this spirit, which had appeared to Moses in the burning bush as the 'I AM', was approaching the earth. They sensed that the Kingdom of Heaven was near.

John had experienced something like this in his prenatal existence. We read in Luke's gospel how he leapt in the womb of his mother, Elizabeth, at the approach of the Nathan Jesus in the womb of the heavenly Mary. We must not take this encounter symbolically but literally. Here the profound connection between John and Jesus is expressed. The Adam soul in the yet unborn John found in the yet unborn Nathan Jesus its higher soul being or sister soul from which it had been separated by the Fall. Early painters often portrayed John and Jesus together with Mary, based on a correct feeling for this belonging together. Most likely, however, the children grew up far away from each other, and it is doubtful that they were ever together during the years of their childhood and youth.

Into the Nathan Jesus, the sister soul of Adam, the Christ spirit would descend to redeem Adam's guilt. Since the Fall and thanks to the adversary powers, the 'old' human being had become detached from its origins and risked becoming spiritually unfruitful. It needed to be rescued by the 'new' human being. In the future, human beings will no longer be clothed in a physical body but in a new spiritual body, a resurrection body. But the creation of this new spiritual body could only be achieved by the highest divine being in and through a human sheath that was in a certain sense free of sin – in other words, in and through the body of Jesus of Nazareth.

The old human being, Adam-John, performed the deed by which the Christ Being was begotten in the guiltless heavenly human being of Jesus. From that point on, we learn, John must 'decrease', while the new human being must 'increase' (Jn 3:30). Just as the light and strength of the outer sun decreases past its high point in June until it reaches its low point in the winter, at which time the inwardly germinating sun-being can be born in the soul, so John, born in midsummer, gave way to the sun-spirit that must increase. John was the highest bearer of the spirit of the Old Testament. Out of him spoke for the last time the power of revelation from the past: an angel spoke through him because the truly free power of the I was given to human beings only through Christ.

John, who is the 'old', the 'last', points to the 'first', the 'new', who comes after him, who is mightier than he, and whose sandal straps he is not worthy to stoop down and untie (Mk 1:7). John baptised with water, but the Christ will baptise with the Holy Spirit.

When we recall that the two men had been together at the Essene settlement before meeting at the Jordan, we might wonder whether John had perhaps already recognised in his cousin the future bearer of the Messiah, and whether the primeval bond between the Adam soul and its sister had been awakened again. I would suggest that this was not the case. At that time the Zarathustra I, which had originally been incarnated in the Solomon Jesus, was still working in the Nathan Jesus. Because of this, the sister soul of Adam did not show itself in its original heavenly nature, but was instead permeated with initiation wisdom and the accumulated experience of many lives.

After the conversation with his stepmother, when Jesus

made his way to John the Baptist, the Zarathustra I had withdrawn from his body. He had returned to his original state in a sense, and as a result the extraordinarily strong attraction that existed between the souls of John and the Nathan Jesus became active again.

Matthew relates that when Jesus appeared asking to be baptised, John tried to deter him, wanting instead to be baptised by him. But Jesus replied that it had to happen 'to fulfil all righteousness [Greek: *dikaiosunē*]' (Mt 3:15 NIV). John performed the baptism, and when Jesus emerged from the water the heavens opened and the spirit of God descended on him like a dove. A voice from heaven was heard speaking words that, with slight variations, are found in all four gospels (Mt 3:17, Mk 1:9–11, Lk 3:21–22, and Jn 1:32–34) and which are usually translated as: 'This is my beloved Son, with whom I am well pleased,' or in the Letter to the Hebrews (1:5): 'You are my Son, today I have begotten you.'

John Madsen, again following indications from Rudolf Steiner, translates these words as 'This is my Son whom I love; in him will I reveal myself' (Mt 3:17). This is a most remarkable indication of the Jordan mystery, and one I will return to later. The gospels express this mystery in simple words, but how can we understand what happened here?

In the first place it is important to view this event as an objective, historical fact, even though any outer proof of it is lacking. Roman historians of the time did not mention this event, and we cannot regard later Christian writings as historical documents in the usual sense. As we have seen, these are mystery books and not historical chronicles. It is therefore a question that has always been viewed as one of faith. Rudolf Steiner speaks in this case of a 'mystical fact': an objective, historical event, but one whose full significance can only be comprehended through profound spiritual experience.

Over the course of time, however, the central importance of the baptism in the Jordan was forgotten. One indication of this is that the date of the baptism, January 6, was no longer celebrated as the day of Christ's 'birth', but as the adoration of the Magi following the birth of Jesus on December 25. This is connected with the fact that Jesus and Christ came to be considered as identical and, as a result, the birth of Jesus was equated with the birth of God's Son. The epiphany of Christ descending on Jesus at the baptism was replaced by the epiphany of the three kings worshipping at the feet of the holy infant.

It is my profound conviction, however, that insight into what took place at the baptism of Jesus in the Jordan is essential to understanding Christianity.

To understand what happened when ordinary people were baptised by John in the Jordan, we must refer to the spiritual-scientific view of the human being – something we have alluded to already in this chapter. According to this view, human beings possess a physical body, an etheric or life body, an astral body, which we can also simply call the soul, and finally the I, the individuality or spiritual core of the human being that uses the other three bodies as its vehicle or instrument. We can also say that the I clothes itself in three sheaths or garments, which it then lays aside one by one at death, for not only the physical and etheric bodies fall away, the transitory part of the astral body also dissolves at a certain point after death.[1]

As mentioned before, when John submerged those who came to be baptised by him in the Jordan, their etheric body along with their I and astral bodies partially detached themselves from the physical body. This was a kind of dying process, which caused the life tableau to unroll. In Jesus, however, only the three garments of the I were present, because the Zarathustra I had departed these three sheaths shortly before. These sheaths were the original physical, etheric and astral bodies of the Nathan Jesus – his mortal nature, which from the beginning was of an exceptional character because this was a heavenly child from a heavenly mother. From the father's side the forming of this human being was determined by the priestly element: the ancestors of Joseph, the carpenter, had led lives of piety and soberness; they had been 'righteous ones'. In addition, since Jesus's birth the nirmanakaya of the Buddha, his spiritual radiance, had been at work in Jesus's astral body.

In this pure human vessel – totally unique in the development of humanity – the Zarathustra-I had worked for eighteen years. This had ennobled this vessel to an even more profound degree, through the wisdom and knowledge of one of the greatest initiates, and through the pain for humanity that had been transformed into love and the deepest compassion.

Thus, Jesus stood before John ready to receive the Christ spirit into himself. A being of the very highest divinity took the place in Jesus that in an ordinary human being is filled by the I, the individual spirit. This highest I-being, the I of humanity, worked for three years in the sheaths of Jesus of Nazareth. During that time these three mortal garments were transformed into the resurrection body of Jesus, who had become Jesus Christ. After the resurrection, the distinction between Jesus the human being and Christ the Son of God can no longer be made.

7

Signs and Sayings

With the help of Rudolf Steiner's spiritual science, we have tried to explain some enigmatic aspects of Jesus. But what of the Christ? Who is he? To this question John the Evangelist gives the clearest answer. John calls Christ the Logos, the Word and says: 'All things were made through him, and without him was not anything made that was made' (Jn 1:3). John thus views Christ as the creator who creates out of his unity with the Father God. He is the revelation of the Hidden One and is therefore called the Son.

Through their star wisdom the ancient Egyptians had already observed the cosmic sun spirit, whom they worshipped as Osiris, drawing near to the earth. They saw how he approached from the realm of the fixed stars (symbolised by the constellation of Orion), passing through the planetary spheres and into the elements of fire, air and water. Moses, who as the adopted son of the Pharaoh was initiated into the Egyptian mysteries of Osiris and Isis, was initiated even more deeply into the spiritual wisdom of the earth by the Midianite initiate Jethro, with whom Moses stayed for forty years after his flight from Egypt.[1]

The sun spirit revealed itself to Moses in the fire of the burning bush, in the water he struck from the rocks, and in the cloud and smoke phenomena that guided the Israelites through the desert – all of which were connected with the earth. Moses and his brother, Aaron, however, could not yet distinguish that it was the Christ being who revealed himself in the elements. They still identified him with Yahweh, the god of the Jewish people.[2] For this reason they were not allowed to enter the Promised Land (Nm 20–12); both of them died before the people reached the eastern bank of the Jordan.

In the revelation of the burning bush the Godhead made itself known to Moses as the 'I AM'. This is the name that is unpronounceable because you can only say 'I am' to yourself, not to someone else. The secret of the Christ name, which in the Gospel of John is expressed in the seven 'I AM' sayings (see pp. 98ff), points to the most individual aspect in every human being: the I. Christ is the God who brings the full reality of the I to human beings. It is only because of this that human beings can find their earthly destiny, which lies in the development of freedom and love. This is also the source of all future developments.

In former cultural epochs, divine beings had also made use of human beings to guide humanity on earth. Greek heroes and demigods had always been human beings that were indwelt by higher spiritual beings. When in the *Epic of Gilgamesh* we read that Gilgamesh is one third human and two thirds divine, something very definite is meant by this, it is not just pretty imagery.[3] These indwelling 'gods' were of a higher order than human beings; they were beings from the hierarchy of the angels or archangels. But although they were able to permeate the spiritual bodies of human beings, they were never able to descend all the way down into the physical body. For this reason, these higher beings could never experience what every human being has to experience: death. Death has to do with the material density of the physical body which, as described by the Fall, was caused by the intervention of Luciferic and Ahrimanic powers.

In order to perform his deed of redemption for humanity, Christ had to overcome death. He had to remove the influence of Lucifer and Ahriman, who keep human beings in the grip of death, from the body of the human being into whom he descended – Jesus of Nazareth. He had to penetrate down into the densest parts of the physical body, into the skeleton itself, and there drive out the 'ruler of this world'. He was the first and only god able to do this. In the spiritual world, death was unknown. No god had ever gone through human death. In Jesus the highest god, the creative Logos, experienced the dying process that must be transformed and re-enlivened into a new creation.

The Christ being was known to the initiates in the ancient mysteries as the great sun spirit, the leading spirit of our world that had worked creatively from the beginning. It was this being that connected itself with Jesus. The writer of the Gospel of John connects the beginning of his gospel with the beginning of the Old Testament where it is written: 'And the spirit of God was moving over the waters. And God said: "Let there be light." And there was light' (Gn 1:2f). The divine spirit speaks the creative Word through the world. John echoes this in his opening lines when he writes: 'In the beginning was the Word.'

When the Word speaks, light comes about. In the Word, therefore, was life, for otherwise nothing could come into existence through it. The gospel says: 'In the Word was life, and life was the light of humanity' (Jn 1:4).

The same spirit of God that hovered over the waters, hovered over the waters of the Jordan and descended into Jesus: 'And the Word became flesh and lived among us' (Jn 1:14).

As a transcendent cosmic being, Christ could only be experienced outside of the body, either through initiation or in the spiritual world after death. With the baptism, however, Christ brought the Kingdom of Heaven down into the human being. This means that since that time, those who take Christ into their hearts are able to experience this heavenly kingdom in their own I without having to leave their body.

Over the course of time, however, the cosmic aspect of the Christ being has received less attention; in a new Christology this aspect must be rediscovered. It will help to view Christianity as the *deeds* of a cosmic being, and not just a body of teachings or doctrines *about* that being. In his book *The Philosophy of Mythology,* the German philosopher Friedrich Schelling says:

> The actual content of Christianity is exclusively the person of Christ. Christ is not the teacher as is usually said. Christ is not the founder, he is the content of Christianity.[4]

In the short space available here it is my intention to highlight only a few important events that mark Christ's life on earth, in the hope that the interested reader will find in them a guide for further study.[5]

After the baptism, Jesus did not return home straight away, but was led into the desert by the spirit (the Greek words *eis ten eremon* can also mean 'into the loneliness'). It is important to form a clear picture of this first stage, which must be understood purely as an inner experience. We are too quickly inclined to imagine the temptation in the desert, which follows the baptism, as an outer scene, as though the devil came to Jesus in a physical form. But here a spiritual experience is described that Jesus underwent in his soul.

What makes the temptation remarkable is that you might have expected it to occur when Jesus was still just a human being, and that once the baptism had taken place, the God in him would have made all approaches by the evil powers impossible. But that is not so. For while these temptations do echo what Jesus lived through prior to the baptism, they only force themselves onto him when the spirit is at the very beginning of its work in him. The Epistle to the Hebrews says in this connection:

> For we do not have a High Priest who cannot suffer our weaknesses with us. He made himself like us and endured the same temptations in everything, only he remained free of sin. (Heb 4:15)

The possibility of going astray is part of being human. It was not the intention of the Christ to evade being human, but rather to experience it in its depths, and temptation was an inherent part of this. This inner experience, which Christ underwent in the lonely, barren desert of Judea is mentioned by the gospel writers in a few lines: Matthew and Luke give a fuller description of it, whereas Mark is extremely concise and John doesn't mention the scene at all.

And yet, this inner event is incredibly significant, because it contains the seed from which the betrayal by Judas and the crucifixion itself will sprout. To understand this, we must return to the pictures of this event found in the Akashic Record and described by Rudolf Steiner in *The Fifth Gospel.* These pictures correspond with the content of the gospel texts, only the sequence of the three temptations is different.

The evangelists use two words to indicate the tempters: 'diabolos', which is usually translated as 'Devil', and 'satanas' or Satan. We will see that two different beings are indeed meant by these names and that we have already encountered them: they are Lucifer (diabolos) and Ahriman (satanas). These two beings approached Jesus in turn, each according to their nature, and then joined together to attack him.

During the forty days of loneliness, and also for a certain time thereafter, Christ lived in the memories of the experiences Jesus had gone through in the last eighteen years. He beheld the impressions preserved in Jesus's astral body of Lucifer and Ahriman fleeing from the gates of the Essene settlements to other people. According to Steiner, Christ felt attracted to these figures because they are the powers that human beings must fight on earth. Now, dwelling for the first time in a human body, he joined the battle against Lucifer and Ahriman.

The scenes that follow the forty days in the desert are described somewhat differently by Rudolf Steiner according to the Fifth Gospel, the Akashic Record, than in the four canonical gospels. This should not lead us to conclude that only one or the other can be true. As has already been mentioned, different viewpoints complement each other, allowing us to construct a broader and more detailed picture. This especially holds true when it comes to spiritual observations. The four gospels indicate the main aspects of events, while the

Fifth Gospel provides a more general picture as well as an explanation of them. Rudolf Steiner called the Fifth Gospel the Gospel of *Erkenntnis,* the Gospel of Knowledge and Insight. Rudolf Steiner describes the three temptations in the opposite order to how they are related by Matthew and Luke.

Lucifer, the spirit of pride and self-importance, was the first to approach Christ inwardly. He described the delights of the Luciferic realm that would seduce every human being who had even the smallest bit of hubris in him. Then he said: 'I will give you power over everything you see, the earthly and even the forces beyond the earthly. For the power belongs to me, and I can give it to whom I will. If you will kneel in worship of me, the whole world shall be yours.' (Lk 4:6–7)

But Christ knew Lucifer. There was nothing in him that corresponded with Lucifer's world, and so he was able to turn aside the latter's attack.

Lucifer then undertook a second attack, but now with the support of Ahriman. Lucifer wanted to light the false fire of hubris in Jesus Christ, and Ahriman wanted to make use of his fear. Lucifer offered to help Jesus Christ overcome the weight of the material body and counteract the laws of gravity. He can throw himself off the parapet of the Temple without being killed. Ahriman then said: 'I will protect you from your fear. Throw yourself down!'

Both were urging him on, but because they kept each other in balance and thereby neutralised each other's power, Christ was able to stand up to their attack and display the strength that human beings must find on earth if they are to overcome Lucifer and Ahriman.

Ahriman then sent Lucifer away as a hindrance to his own efforts. He approached Jesus Christ alone and said:

'Command these stones to become bread.' In other words, change the mineral content of the stones – their metal content – into money so that people can buy bread to feed themselves.

Christ replied: 'The human being does not live by bread alone, but by that which nourishes him from the divine world.' Christ knew this because he had descended from this high, sustaining divinity to the earth. But he did not yet know the earth the way Ahriman knows it. And so Ahriman replied: 'You may be right, but you only know what holds true in spiritual heights. You have never before been on the earth. Down here people have an urgent need for stones to be changed into bread. For they cannot feed themselves only with spirit.'

The Christ being, who had only just descended to the earth, did not know that on earth it is necessary to change material substance (metal, money) into bread. Ahriman pointed out to him that people on earth need money to pay for their bread, that money feeds them. On this point he was correct, and so Christ was unable to completely repel his attack.[6]

From this unresolved question of the stones and the bread, Ahriman retained the mortal sting that would allow him to inflict death on Jesus Christ, and this sting was the power of money. Judas betrayed Christ for thirty pieces of silver. Christ had to admit the power of money into the circle of his disciples – bread needed to be bought, and Judas kept the purse – and by the power of money, Ahriman was able to gain access to one of his closest disciples. In the Gospel of John, we read that Satan took possession of Judas, prompting him to commit the betrayal that led to Jesus Christ's execution.[7] By this, however, the highest good was accomplished: namely, the sacrificial death of the saviour. Ahriman's evil intention succeeded, but without realising it, he had put himself in the service of the highest good. The Mystery of Golgotha took place, in part, because of his help.

Jesus Christ returned to Galilee and resumed his work as a carpenter. He pondered in his soul the words Ahriman had spoken to him about the need for people to change stones into bread and the serious question this raised. Because of this, Christ did not go to the scribes and leaders of the people, nor to the pious and righteous ones, but to the people he had met earlier through his work, the ones the Bible calls publicans and sinners. These were the ones who had to toil in order to buy bread and who therefore had to change stones into bread. He realised that this preoccupation with making money and the hardness of physical life had made human beings egotistic, alienating them from the Kingdom of God and causing them to slip into the power of Ahriman.

The people with whom Christ spent time outwardly saw the same Jesus of Nazareth they had known before, the same loving and compassionate person who had sat with them after work and had consoled them. But was he the same? From his face there now shone a stronger radiance, and when he came to them they felt not only consoled but healed. He drove out the demons that caused people to suffer and were making them ill, the same demons who had taken the place of the holy gods on the pagan altars. These demons were the first to recognise and acknowledge him:

> In the synagogue at Capernaum a man with an unclean spirit suddenly cried out: 'What is between us and you, Jesus, you Nazarene? You have come to destroy us.

> I know who you are, you are the Holy One of God.' Then Jesus spoke sternly to him, 'Be silent and leave him!' And the unclean spirit threw the man this way and that; then it left him with loud shouts and cries. (Mk 1:23–26)

In Jesus's memory lived the experience of what he went through at the pagan altar when he heard words spoken from the cosmic heights describing the decline of humanity. Now, the Christ in him knew that he had to prepare the way upwards, helping human beings to find the spirit again. He thus reworked the words he had heard spoken at the pagan altar, reversing the sequence line by line and inverting their meaning, to create what we know as the Lord's Prayer.

He placed the last line, 'You Fathers in the heavens', at the beginning and changed it to 'Our Father in the heaven', no longer referring to the multiplicity of hierarchical beings, but instead to the highest Father God. The line in the middle, 'experienced in the daily bread', which is connected with the physical embodiment of human beings and Ahriman's secret regarding bread and the money needed to buy it, was changed into an appeal for bread. It became a stimulus for human beings to regard bread as a gift from God, and not just as a material, unspiritual piece of food. And so on, throughout the entire prayer.

> Amen.
> The evils hold sway,
> Witness of egoity releasing itself.
> Selfhood guilt through others incurred,

Experienced in the daily bread,
Wherein the will of the heavens does not rule,
Because man separated himself from your realm,
And forgot your names,
You Fathers in the heavens.

Our Father in the heavens,
Hallowed be your name,
Your kingdom come, your will be done,
On Earth as it is in the heavens.
Give us today our daily bread,
Forgive us our trespasses, as we forgive
those who trespass against us
And lead us not into temptation,
But deliver us from evil.
Amen.

From this point on, I will draw on the Gospel of John in describing the life of Jesus Christ.

We are used to speaking of the miracles that Christ performed, and we find seven of these so-called miracles described in John's gospel, beginning with the marriage in Cana and ending with the raising of Lazarus. As I mentioned in the foreword to this book, we need not speak of miracles in the sense of divine magic or anything like it. Instead, it is better to use the word 'signs' here. The seven signs mark the seven stages in which the power and effect of Christ working in Jesus of Nazareth increases – the number seven always points to a process taking place in time.

Concurrently, however, there is a counter movement that comes to expression through an increasing weakening. The divine being as it penetrated deeper into the being of Jesus of Nazareth deified his humanness. But at the same time, in becoming human, the Christ had to make himself smaller. He had to let go of his cosmic power in order, as a servant, to experience the deepest point of human powerlessness: the total suffering of the human condition in the extreme bitterness of humiliation, torture and death.

Accompanying these seven signs are the seven 'I AM' sayings, in which Christ expressed aspects of his own being. They are like seven trumpets that sound forth in the dramatic development of his life; at the same time, they also serve as mighty imaginations filled with an unprecedented active force. For those who take these words into the depths of their soul, they are a way of intuitively experiencing the Christ.

We will now look at the seven signs and then go on to a brief contemplation on the seven I AM sayings. According to John the seven signs Christ gives are:

- The marriage in Cana, where water was changed into wine (2:1–11)
- The healing of the son of a nobleman in Capernaum in Galilee (4:46–54)
- The healing on the Sabbath of the man who had been paralysed for thirty-eight years by the Pool of Bethesda (5:1–18)
- The feeding of the five thousand by the Sea of Galilee (6:1–15)
- Jesus walking on the water (6:16–21)
- Healing the man born blind in Jerusalem, also on the Sabbath (9:1–41)
- The raising of Lazarus in Bethany in Judea (11:1–44)

The Christ spirit had not penetrated very far into the bodily being of Jesus when the marriage in Cana took place. In order to give this sign, he therefore had to make use of the bond that connected him with his mother.

In ancient times, the power and effectiveness of spiritual deeds was mediated by the bonds of blood. By marrying within one's own bloodline one preserved the possibility of attaining clairvoyant perception and of working effectively on other human beings, what we might call a kind of soul magic. This was the basis of all healing. In the Jewish people, clairvoyance and the concomitant soul magic had declined, but blood relationships were still nurtured and preserved. The experience of the Jewish people's collective consciousness could be summed up in the words, 'I and Father Abraham are one.' They felt strongly the bonds of blood that connected them to their ancestor, Abraham. In Galilee, however, this close blood relationship was no longer as strongly present; the people there had married outside of family bloodlines.

Christ came to the earth to awaken self-consciousness in the individual human being, regardless of blood relationships. The people in Galilee were therefore more suited than those in Judea to receive his first sign. According to Rudolf Steiner, if in the distant past wine had run out at a wedding, the guests would have been able to experience the water they were then given as wine because of the magical power of the blood relationship that connected those present at the celebration. This could only happen, however, if the right relationship created a bond among those who sought to achieve this magical effect and those who were open to receiving it. The latter then received the water as if it were really wine.

This is what Christ brought about in the wedding guests

in Cana through the spiritual power that streamed from him, even though no blood bond connected him to the guests. It was a new power, one that proceeded from the divine I that existed before Abraham (as Christ says later while teaching in the temple courts, 'Before Abraham was, I am' – Jn 8:58). But this power could not yet fully work. It still needed the help of the soul element that worked in Mary, his mother. She is the one who called her son's attention to the fact that there was no more wine. Christ then answered: '*Ti emoi kai soi gynai; oupō hēkei he ōra mou.*' The first part of this sentence is usually translated as 'Woman, why do you involve me?' (NIV), which sounds as though Christ was rebuking his mother, and makes no sense with regards to what follows. Mary told the servants to do whatever Christ tells them. He told them to pour water into six stone jars that were standing nearby. The servants then gave the master of ceremonies a drink from those jars. To him, the water tasted of wine, and so it does subsequently to the other guests.

It is strange that those theologians and Bible critics who are able to read Greek leave this nonsense in the text. *Ti emoi kai soi* literally means 'What to me and to you', which could be rendered as: 'What is there between you and me?' That is not a rebuke, but something that is meant positively. Christ was pointing to what connected him to Mary in such a way that it brought about this magical effect, which he could not yet bring about by himself because 'my hour has not yet come' (*oupō hēkei he hōra mou*).

The Christ-'I' evoked in the wedding guests in Galilee – where the bride and bridegroom were not of the same blood – an effect similar to wine. Wine originally aroused the power of the I. Human beings did not experience a loss of the I as happens now, but the divinity streaming through them. By drinking wine they rose, as it were, to their I. This is what the disciples experienced: 'What Jesus did here in Cana of Galilee was the first of the signs through which he revealed his glory; and his disciples believed in him' (Jn 2:11 NIV).

With the second sign, the healing of the son of a nobleman, Christ's power had grown. The nobleman came to him in distress because his son was dying. Christ said to him: 'Your son will live,' and the man believed him and departed (Jn 4:50 NIV). At that moment, we are told, the child's fever went down and he was healed.

Here it is the power of faith which, together with the Christ power, brings about the healing. If the father had not believed, the son would not have been healed. It therefore still required two souls – those of Jesus and the nobleman – to create the effect, but the power of faith was evoked in the nobleman directly by Christ. At the wedding in Cana, the soul element of the mother was still needed to open the souls of the wedding guests to the working of the spirit.

In the third sign the working of the spirit became even stronger. A paralysed man who had been unable to walk for thirty-eight years, was lying on a bed by the Pool of Bethesda. From time to time an angel stirred the water and whoever was the first to step into the pool was healed from whatever illness they had. The man, however, had no one to help him into the water, and so he had lain there in vain for a long time.

On the day Christ encountered the man it was the Sabbath and there was a festive mood of joy and love. Christ on seeing the man said: 'Stand up, take your pallet and walk!' (Jn 5:8). Immediately the man was healed and he took up his pallet and left. The Jews were surprised to see him, not because he was healed but because he was carrying his pallet on the Sabbath, which was not allowed.

Jesus met the man later in the Temple and said to him: 'See, you have become well. Sin no more, that your destiny will bring you nothing worse' (Jn 5:14). The man's affliction was therefore connected with his sin. Whether it was something he did in his present life or in a prior one is not important. What is revealing about this sign is that the power of Christ was now able to heal not only a physical ailment, but also to work into the depths of the soul of the other person and remedy a moral defect. This time no one else was needed for it, which was still the case in the two previous signs. On the Sabbath, God gives strength to human souls, which Christ was able to transfer to the paralysed man.

The fourth sign is the feeding of the five thousand by the Sea of Galilee. Now the Christ power had increased to such an extent that Christ was able to share it with his disciples: the five barley loaves and two fishes are 'increased'. In other words, because he divided them with thanks and gave them to his disciples, the nourishing Christ power streamed through the souls of the disciples to the assembled people. They were satisfied in the same way as at the marriage in Cana, where the guests tasted the water as wine and felt the effects of wine.

In the fifth sign the disciples saw Jesus 'walking on the sea' (Jn 6:19). As I described in the foreword, this was explained to me as a supersensible experience that the disciples had while asleep at night. The experience of the feeding of the five thousand had sunk down into their souls and they had become clairvoyant in their sleep. They beheld Jesus as a spiritual being 'walking on the sea'. They were afraid, but Christ calmed them. He came on board and immediately they reached land, meaning they woke up (Jn 6:21).[8] The power that now emanated from Christ was such that it awakened supersensory perception within his disciples who were then able to behold him in his spiritual form.

The next sign is the healing of the man born blind. Here, too, the various established translations make understanding this moving passage difficult. For instance, the Revised Standard Version reads:

> As [Christ] passed by, he saw a man blind from his birth. And his disciples asked him, 'Rabbi, who sinned, this man or his parents, that he was born blind?' Jesus answered, 'It was not that this man sinned, or his parents, but that the works of God might be made manifest in him.' (Jn 9:1–3)

Then he healed the man.

What interpretation does the formulation of the last sentence suggest? The man himself had not sinned that he had to pay for it with blindness and neither had his parents. God therefore let someone be born blind, with all the suffering it causes, just so that Christ could heal him. For the glory of God a 'miracle' is allowed to happen, but apparently God's miraculous power can only become manifest after he has first made a human being miserable. That is a rather questionable and certainly not very 'Christian' way of thinking.

In the original Greek, the last sentence reads: *hina phanerotē ta erga tou theou en autō,* 'so that the works of the God become manifest in him.' Now, *tou theou* may also be translated as 'of the god' or 'of the divine', without the definite article. It is open to interpretation whether the meaning refers to God in heaven, or to the divine in the human being. In this context, I believe that *ho theos en autō* means 'the divine in him', not 'God in heaven'.

Jesus's words from the tenth chapter of the Gospel of John can help us better understand this statement. In a sharp dispute with the Jews in the Temple in Jerusalem, he reminded them of the words in Psalm 82:6: 'You are gods.' In the innermost core of the human being there lives something that is of the same divine substance as God; we call that innermost being in ourselves our I, our individuality. This I does not come from our father and mother or from our ancestors, nor is it the same as the personality we are in this life. The personality is but one of the forms in which our individual I expresses itself. The latter goes from one earthly embodiment to another, dwelling for a certain time in spiritual realms in between.

The blindness of the man born blind was the consequence of something his I had done or left undone in a prior life: *ta erga tou theou en autō,* the works of the divine (the I) in him had become manifest in the phenomenon of his blindness in his current life. Neither his parents nor the earthly personality (that he expresses as 'I') did something that resulted in his blindness. It was the divine in himself.

With this, Christ pointed to the law of karma and the balancing of destiny. The fact that this person could be healed of his blindness meant that the power of Christ had further increased and was able to work even more deeply. He penetrated into the eternal I of the other human being, into that which transcends birth and death. With his own 'I AM', his own divinity, he touched the divinity of the blind man and in so doing bestowed upon him the strength to overcome the consequences of his own works.

This sixth sign caused an even greater agitation among the scribes and Pharisees than the previous signs did. They felt their authority was being challenged, first by the man who had been born blind and who, following his healing by Christ, stood up to their insistent and increasingly abusive questioning, and then by Christ himself in the debate they had with him in the tenth chapter of John's gospel. The tension of the I-drama increased, and with the seventh sign, the raising of Lazarus, it intensified to the point that the Sanhedrin (the assembly of Jewish leaders) decided to kill Jesus.[9]

With the raising of Lazarus, we come to a central motif in the development of Rudolf Steiner's spiritual investigations. When Steiner published his basic work on Christianity in 1902, *Christianity as Mystical Fact,* he described this event in such a way that we can speak of a kind of key point in his Christology. The raising from the dead is explained by Steiner as an initiation performed on Lazarus by Christ.

Moreover, in Steiner's book it is pointed out for the first time that Lazarus was the 'disciple Jesus loved', and after being raised from the grave he was given the name John. The writer of the gospel himself went through this initiation, and on him the highest of the seven signs was performed. The Christ power permeated one of the disciples in such a way that from that moment on he became a different human being – a Christ-permeated human being. At the same time, with the raising of Lazarus, Christ carried out an act that in the old mysteries had sealed the initiation of the *myste.*

In the gospel, Christ says, 'Lazarus, come out!' (Jn 11:43). In the ancient mysteries this was the command spoken by the hierophant – the high priest of the mystery centre – to call the *myste* back to life from their initiation death of three and a half days. Jesus Christ performed this deed openly as the hierophant of humanity and in so doing brought the old mysteries to an end. The so-called 'mystical death', which the *myste* underwent in the final phase of initiation, now belonged to the past. Lazarus-John was the last person to undergo this old initiation, but he was also the first to be initiated by Christ himself.

What further provoked the scribes and Pharisees is that the raising of Lazarus did not take place in secret away from the eyes of the profane, as in the old mysteries, but openly, in front of Lazarus's sisters, Martha and Mary, and others. This was viewed by the Jewish people as a betrayal of the mysteries, which was punishable by death. However, Christ did not betray the mysteries; what arose in Lazarus through his initiation remained hidden in his innermost being. What Christ did do was make the sacred process of initiation visible. By doing this he indicated that the form of the old mysteries had come to an end and in Lazarus-John something entirely new had been brought about.

What happened in this age-old mystery rite? After a long period of purification and learning, the *myste* reached a stage where they were able to absorb higher spiritual experiences not only into their soul or astral body, but also into their etheric body, which is what could lead to lasting clairvoyance. At this point they were brought into a condition that resembled death and which lasted for three and a half days. The higher members of the human being, the astral and etheric bodies, were partially separated from the physical body, creating a condition that otherwise only occurs at death when this separation becomes permanent. Because of their preparation, when the *myste* returned to their physical body they were able to recall the spiritual experiences they had undergone in the spiritual realm during the three days and nights of their initiation. Their 'initiation sleep' did not bring about the loss of consciousness that usually occurs in the case of normal sleep.

Before Christ, initiation could only take place outside of the body. The etheric body had to be pulled partly out of the physical body in order to receive impressions from the astral body. Initiation sleep was not without danger, however, for if the procedure was disturbed in some way, then death could occur. Moreover, the *myste* had to surrender their own being completely into the hands of the hierophant; they had no freedom at all. By contrast, the new Christian initiation takes place within the body when the Christian candidate allows themselves to be completely permeated by the fire of the blood. This is the baptism given by Christ, not a submersion in water, but a permeation with inner spiritual fire.

So what happened within Lazarus?

According to Steiner, Lazarus was the 'rich young man' who was told that it is easier for a camel to go through the eye of a needle than for a rich man to enter the Kingdom of Heaven (Mt 19:16–26 and Mk 10:17–27). He was deeply moved by his encounter with Christ and became the 'disciple Jesus loved'. This is an expression from the ancient mysteries that was used to indicate a student who understood the intentions and teachings of the Master more profoundly than other followers. The legend says that the rich young man gave away his wealth and followed Jesus. This 'wealth' may not necessarily have consisted of earthly goods. The young man probably possessed the wealth of the ancient mystery wisdom, which he had to sacrifice in order to receive the new Christ mystery.

A peculiar change then occurred, which outwardly seemed to be an illness. Lazarus's sisters were concerned and sent a message to Jesus. He replied: 'This illness does not lead to death but to the revelation of God; the creative might of the Son of God shall be revealed through it' (Jn 11:4). The word *doxa* in the Greek text is usually translated as 'glory' ('for the glory of God'), but the word 'glory' has lost some of its power as 'the light of revelation of God'.

Jesus did not immediately go to heal his friend but waited a few days before going to Bethany to 'awaken' Lazarus. That which used to be accomplished by the hierophant, namely the loosening of the higher members from the physical body of the *myste,* happened here at a distance through the working of Christ in Lazarus. Lazarus had died and was laid in his grave. Then the fourth day came, when the awakening took place and Jesus gave his most profound sign.

Christ found in the one he loves the disciple through whom he was able to reveal his being. Because of his initiation, Lazarus became John, the author of the fourth gospel. In this gospel we find the seven 'I AM' sayings that, in a certain respect, correspond with the parables of the other three gospels. They contain the essence of Christ's being, and therefore of Christianity itself. The seven 'I AM' sayings are:

1. I AM the bread of life (6:35)
2. I AM the light of the world (8:12)
3. I AM the door (10:7)
4. I AM the good shepherd (10:14)

5. I AM the resurrection and the life (11:25)
6. I AM the way, the truth, and the life (14:6)
7. I AM the true vine (15:1)

In contemplating these sayings, we must take into consideration at what moments, in what context, and to whom they are spoken.

'I am the bread of life' was spoken to the people after the feeding of the five thousand when Christ revealed himself as the lord of the earth. His sun spirit had now penetrated so far into the earthly body of Jesus that this spirit could enter via him into the disciples. The people (representing all of humanity) received the bread as nourishment that does not come from transitory sources but bears eternal life in it. Christ connected himself as a cosmic sun being with the earth; he became the spirit of the earth and the earth became his 'body'. When we walk over the earth we tread on his body with our feet. Earthly bread bears his spiritual working if it is blessed and divided in his name.

'I am the light of the world' was also spoken before a crowd of people following the scene with the adulteress, and points to Christ as the lord of destiny. A woman who had been caught in adultery was brought before Christ by the scribes and Pharisees who asked him what they should do with her. The punishment for adultery according to the law of Moses was to be stoned to death. As Christ listened, he made marks in the sand, meaning he wrote the woman's guilt into the earth. In a subsequent life the woman will have to compensate for her guilt by her karma. But Christ did not condemn her, instead he reminded her of her freedom: 'Go, and from now on do not sin any more' (Jn 8:11). In freedom, out of insight, a person can say 'No' to temptation and the urge to sin. Karma brings about the balancing of destiny through the light of wisdom in the world, not through punishment. Christ is the lord of karma and the bringer of freedom, the light of the world, so that love can work among human beings.

The next two 'I AM' sayings – 'I am the door' and 'I am the good shepherd' – were spoken to the Pharisees. They were the seducers of the people, the wolves or robbers who did not enter the sheepfold through the door but gained illegitimate entrance to corrupt the sheep (human souls). Christ revealed himself as the vanquisher of evil, but not by destroying this evil. Human beings must recognise the door and the good shepherd in freedom and in that way shut out evil.

'I am the resurrection and the life' was spoken to one person, Martha, just before the raising of her brother, Lazarus, the meaning and significance of which we have already discussed.

The sixth and seventh 'I AM' sayings – 'I am the way, the truth, and the life' and 'I am the true vine' – Christ spoke to his disciples: to Thomas, the doubter, and to the twelve on Maundy Thursday.

By means of the seventh sign, the raising of Lazarus from his initiation sleep, Christ showed that his power brings about the resurrection of human beings, allowing them to fill themselves with eternal life. Those who want to share in this life may feel like twigs or shoots of the vine. They must stay connected with him to bear fruit.

The process of becoming a true human being is a way, a path. Christ is this way, which humanity must travel. Christ is the truth that the spirit of truth (the Holy Spirit) sends as his I to whomever is willing to receive it. This spirit of truth makes us free. I will come back to this in connection with the Pentecost event.

The 'I AM' sayings form a totality that, taken together, presents itself as the mystery of bread and wine. The mystery of bread and wine is the offering of Jesus Christ.

In the next chapter we will try to approach this secret more deeply by considering the crucifixion, death, and resurrection in the light of new spiritual knowledge.

8

The Son of Man and the Transfiguration

Before we can turn our attention to the final act of the great Christ drama, which takes place in the city of Jerusalem, we must first review some terms used in the gospels and one hard to understand sign that is not found in the Gospel of John, namely the transfiguration on Mount Tabor.

First, let us consider the phrases 'Son of Man' and 'Son of God' in the light of spiritual science.

The expression *ho huios tou anthrōpou,* 'the Son of Man', appears numerous times in all four gospels, where, but for one exception, it is spoken only by Jesus Christ. The theological interpretations usually given for this phrase are inadequate. Some claim the phrase refers to the human being in a general sense, making the expression nothing more than a flowery descriptor, others think that Jesus uses this term simply to indicate himself. But again, these words must be understood in the light of mystery wisdom. In mystery language, 'son' does not mean a physical descendant, but instead refers to a spiritual descent, a being that comes into existence out of another being, much like a flower that blossoms on a plant which until that moment had only leaves.[1]

The human being may well be compared with a plant. Here, too, one manifestation develops out of another, just as the flower emerges from the leaf. As we have already discussed in connection with the baptism in the Jordan, the human being consists of a physical body, a life or etheric body, a soul or astral body, and an I. The I works in the three lower bodies guided by higher hierarchical beings in such a way that three aspects of the soul develop out of them. As well as occurring in the individual, this unfolding of the soul also corresponds to periods in the development of humanity.

Out of the astral body what is known in anthroposophy as the sentient soul develops. This is the primary realm of the psyche and the seat of such emotions as lust and desire, joy and sorrow, sympathy and antipathy. This part of the soul awakened in humanity in general in Egyptian-Babylonian times, between 3000 and 700 BC. Of course, such sensations and feelings were also present in human beings before those times, but during this period they became more inward and developed a more personally coloured character.

In the next cultural epoch, which encompassed Greek and Roman times and the Middle Ages, the second soul aspect, the intellectual-mind soul, developed out of the etheric body. The deepening inwardness continued and at the same time the power of rational thinking awakened. This was accompanied by a stronger, more clearly defined sense of self. The incarnation of Christ occurred in this epoch.

A third soul aspect still lay in the future for humanity at this point, the consciousness soul. This became active in modern times at the start of the fifteenth century and arose out of the physical body. In the consciousness soul the human I becomes aware of its power and freedom; it represents the highest blossoming of the human psyche. Out of this aspect, the self-conscious I can begin to develop the higher aspects of the human being, but now as a free and autonomous spiritual being. Prior to this it had worked on the development of the three soul aspects under the unconscious guidance of hierarchical powers.

In the epoch when the intellectual soul was unfolding, and even before that, there were human beings who, as initiates, had already acquired the qualities of the consciousness soul. These were called 'Sons of Man'.

The Son of Man is therefore a human being who already bears within themselves the element of the consciousness soul. A passage from the twelfth chapter of the Gospel of John clarifies this. Just after Christ predicted his death and a voice was heard from heaven glorifying the name of the Father, Christ said to an uncomprehending crowd:

> 'This is the hour of decision for the whole world. The ruler of this world will be cast out. When I have been exalted above earthly existence, I will draw all human beings to me.' He said this to indicate the death toward which he was going. Then the people answered him: 'When we were taught the Law we always heard that the Christ remains and leads over into the coming eon; so how can you say that the Son of Man must be raised up? Who is this Son of Man?' And Jesus answered: 'For a short time yet the light is in your midst. Tread your path while you have the light, so that the darkness does not overcome you. Whoever walks in darkness does not know where he is going. While you still have the light, open your

> hearts to the light, so that you may become sons of light.' (Jn 12:31–36)

Here we have a clear indication of the luminous nature of the Son of Man; the consciousness soul in its true essence is the light bearer.

When Jesus asked his disciples: 'Who do men say that the Son of Man is?' (Mt 16:13), he meant: which individuals are 'Sons of Man' or 'light bearers'? The disciples also understood the question in that sense, for they responded: 'Some say John the Baptist, others say Elijah ... or one of the other prophets.' Initiates, therefore, who already bore the higher soul part in themselves. In this regard, Jesus was also a 'Son of Man', but he wanted to point out something special to his disciples.

In the consciousness soul, the highest manifestation of the human psyche, the free human I can unfold even higher aspects of our being. But what does this mean? In the consciousness soul the light of the spirit can shine. When we view this part of the soul as a blossoming flower, we should imagine that this soul flower is also the starting point of a still higher, spiritual budding. In this highest revelation of the human essence, we can again distinguish a threefoldness. When human beings have reached the stage of the consciousness soul, they can develop the first spiritual part of their being, the spirit self or manas, which in Christian esotericism is called the Holy Spirit. Subsequently, in the distant future humanity will develop life spirit or buddhi, and the spirit human or atman. In Christian esotericism these two are called the Son and the Father.

Although this process is a free, creative activity of the I, in which human beings rise to higher levels of existence, they still receive the growth of the spiritual aspects of their being as grace from on high. As those aspects of human beings that culminate in the development of the consciousness soul to form the Son of Man grow upward from below, the higher spiritual aspects of human beings descend on them, as it were, from above out of a divine-spiritual world.

Jesus Christ wanted to awaken his disciples to the question of what has to be born in human beings due to his impulse: 'And who do you say that I am?' (Mt 16:15).

The one who is the representative of the life-bestowing spiritual principle from on high, the Son of the living God, the spirit of life, has to come to human beings to be able to receive the first gift of the spirit self. The Son of Man, who grows from below upwards, takes the Son of God into themselves from on high. The disciples could not easily give this answer, because everything was new for them; their own intellect fell short of seeing the awesome secret that encompasses the whole future development of the human race.

And then Peter said: 'You are the Christ, the Son of the living God.' Deep down in his being, which of course had not yet developed the higher spiritual bodies, he was the first human being who acknowledged what, or rather who, was working in Jesus: the divine being that comes from on high. He could not yet 'know' this out of his own consciousness. Jesus therefore said:

> 'Blessed are you, Simon, son of Jona; you have not received this revelation from the world of the senses, but from the world of my Father in the heavens. And I say to you: you are Peter, the Rock. On this Rock I will build my congregation, and the gates of the abyss shall

> not swallow it up. To you I will give the keys to the kingdom of the heavens. What you bind on the earth shall also be considered bound in the heavens, and what you loose on earth shall also be considered loosed in the heavens.' And with emphasis he told his disciples to tell no one that he was the Christ. (Mt 16:17–20)

How was Peter able to give this answer? Because there worked in him in an extraordinary way those forces that Jesus calls 'my Father in the heavens'. Although the higher spiritual bodies of spirit self, life spirit and spirit human will only develop in the future out of the astral, etheric and physical bodies, they would never be able to develop if the divine creative powers had not laid them into the three lower bodies as seeds. Deep in each human being this divinity has been laid, but it remains hidden in the subconscious; it is completely overwhelmed by that which works out of the 'world of the senses', out of a consciousness that is bound to earthly materiality.

Peter, however, was someone in whom these unconscious divine forces were so strong that he was able to depend on them with confidence. The divine Father spoke in him. That is why the impulse that Christ brings from on high can be established on it.

But then something peculiar happened. After the words quoted here, Christ began to prepare his disciples for the events that were to follow: his journey to Jerusalem and his suffering, death, and resurrection. But Peter didn't want to hear it. He said: 'God forbid, Lord! This shall never happen to you' (Mt 16:22). In that moment the Father power did not work in him anymore; he spoke out of his normal consciousness into which Ahriman-Satan, the spirit of deception, can enter. Jesus Christ rejected his words: 'Get behind me, Satan! You are a stumbling-block to me; you do not have in mind the concerns of God, but merely human concerns' (Mt 16:23 NIV).

Bible critics have great difficulties with this. How could Jesus acknowledge Peter as the foundation of his church one moment and then call him Satan the next? The spiritual viewpoints shown above, however, explain the connection. Moreover, Jesus did not call Peter 'Satan', but instead drove out the deceptive satanic spirit that spoke out of what was all-too-human in him and not out of the Father principle.

The reference to binding and loosing also requires an explanation. When Rudolf Steiner refers to this in his lecture series on the Gospel of Matthew, he first points to the old bond that existed between the Hebrew people and the heavens. Abraham was told that his descendants 'will be ordered according to the stars' (Gn 15:5). This meant that the cosmic ordering that is expressed in the twelvefold zodiac was to be reflected in the twelve tribes of his people. This ordering like the stars worked through the blood relationship; in the three times fourteen generations from Abraham to Jesus cosmic relationships are expressed. What was bound or loosed in the hereditary stream of the Hebrews was determined by heavenly ordering and ordinance.

Christ wanted to point out to his disciples that with his coming to the earth, a new order has to come about that is not based on heredity and a love that binds only through the blood, but on the free association of people who, as Peter did, comprehend out of their higher natures what the Christ being is. Communities can then arise in which the I-conscious bond of love connects individual souls with each other. In such a community the destinies of individual human beings will be carried by their fellow human beings. Also, the 'guilt' of a single person can then be 'loosed', because the community has made it its own karmic debt. Through what Christ has brought down from heaven, such a community can again become a reflection of the 'heavenly order' that was formerly reflected in the blood relationship. According to Steiner:

> This scene of Peter's avowal now begins to reveal an infinitely profound meaning to those who have a dawning understanding of it. It denotes the founding of the humanity of the future – a humanity based upon the Ego-nature in man. What takes place in this intimate conversation between Christ and those who were closest to him, is that Christ transmits the power he himself has brought from the macrocosm to what the disciples are to establish.[2]

We will now turn our attention to an event that follows Peter's confession and the announcement of Christ's impending ordeal: the transfiguration on Mount Tabor. This is recorded in the three synoptic gospels; the Gospel of John makes no mention of it.

Jesus took three disciples, Peter, James and John, with him up Mount Tabor, a holy mountain in the south of Galilee. This is one of those many instances where we must interpret the scene both literally – they did actually go up to the summit of this dome-like mountain – and symbolically, meaning in a spiritual sense. The expressions 'on the mountain', 'at the lake', 'in the house' are mystery expressions, and in the gospels they often indicate moments when an inner spiritual event coincides with an outer action. The real, physical event has at the same time an archetypal character.

'On the mountain' means that a higher level of consciousness is reached. 'At the lake', or generally at the edge of the water, indicates the imaginative condition in which the individual beholds images. This condition of consciousness occurs more easily in this environment, whereas on the heights of mountain tops, the individual is more receptive to inspiration. 'In the house' the connection with higher worlds is more difficult to bring about.

The three disciples mentioned above were chosen to go with Christ 'onto the mountain', because they were most receptive to the deeper secrets that are connected with the being of Christ. Before their clairvoyant eyes appeared the spiritual forms of two figures 'shining white like light itself': the prophet Elijah and Moses, standing on either side of Jesus. They disciples beheld Jesus also transfigured: 'His countenance shone like the sun, and his garments became shining white like light itself' (Mt 17:2); 'And his appearance was transformed before their eyes, and his garments shone radiantly, a shining white, bright beyond all measure, whiter than anyone on earth would be able to make them' (Mk 9:3); 'And while he was still deep in prayer, the appearance of his countenance changed and his garment became gleaming, radiant white' (Lk 9:29).

The disciples saw Christ speak with Moses and Elijah. Peter suggested they build three booths on the mountaintop, one for Jesus, one for Elijah, and one for Moses. A cloud then overshadowed the disciples and they heard a voice from within it say: 'This is my Son, the chosen one, listen to him!'

(Lk 9:35). Matthew has it: 'This is my Son whom I love. In him I have been revealed. Hear his word!' (Mt 17:5)

The three disciples experienced an extremely important moment in the continuing penetration of the body of Jesus of Nazareth by the spirit of Christ. What they clairvoyantly observed was not the Resurrection Body – that would only manifest after the Golgotha event – but the spiritualised etheric body. They saw, therefore, as a special grace, the shining 'light body' in which the Resurrected One would later reveal himself to all disciples, and in which the spiritualised physical body is taken up, as a result of which the wounds from the cross can also be seen.

As Luke reports, the meeting with Moses and Elijah related to the approaching completion of Christ's life in Jerusalem. In this world historic conversation, as Rudolf Steiner calls it, representatives of the two streams of humanity already mentioned in this book met the one who, as cosmic Godhead, brought them together by his deed on Golgotha.

Moses, who in an earlier life was a disciple of the great Persian initiate Zarathustra, represents the kingly stream of wisdom. He had been initiated in different mysteries and was able to bring the wisdom of other cultures into the Hebrew people, thus preparing the general mystery of humanity in the incarnation of Christ.

The prophet Elijah, who as we have seen incarnated as John the Baptist, must be viewed as the representative of the other, the shepherd stream. Rudolf Steiner mentioned that the individuality that lived in Elijah also appeared as Phineas, the grandson of Aaron, the first priest of Israel.[3] Phineas diverted the anger of Yahweh from the people of Israel by killing the man who had taken a woman from another people and been seduced to worship idols (Nm 25:6–9). This priestly figure does not work by wisdom, but by his strength and moral purity.

Phineas-Elijah-John the Baptist is a series of incarnations of an individuality who worked through the centuries to preserve the purity of the mission of the ancient Hebrew people – a purity without which no connection with the Christ spirit could have come about.

In the Book of Revelation the figures of Moses and Elijah are also beheld and indicated by the seer as the two witnesses of Christ and as 'the two olive trees and the two lampstands that stand before the Lord of the earth' (Rv 11:3–12).

This is the world secret that Peter, James and John experienced on Mount Tabor. In the representative figures of Elijah and Moses they saw how the spiritual forces that underpin the entire development of the earth and humanity flow together to unite with the cosmic spirit of Christ. Of course, they did not immediately understand this, but that is how it is with everything that relates to a higher spiritual truth. Only slowly can the soul learn to comprehend what it has beheld.

What the gospels describe really was experienced by the apostles. As the Christ drama approached its culmination, the twelve disciples were led deeper into the great mystery unfolding around them. At the same time, they experienced the trials that form part of every initiation, and as the gospels describe in extremely moving ways, they were not all able to endure these tests. Yet we must realise that these twelve disciples (and the wider circle of seventy that formed around them) were prepared by Christ himself for the mission of spreading Christianity into the world.

We might wonder, therefore, if a relationship already existed between these twelve men before they became Christ's disciples. Admittedly they were all followers of John the Baptist and were baptised in the Jordan by him, and some of them were also related, such as the brothers Simon Peter and Andrew, for instance, and James and John, the sons of Zebedee. But a direct connection between all twelve of them initially did not seem to exist.

But there was a connection. According to the spiritual-scientific investigations of Rudolf Steiner, these twelve individualities had incarnated a century and a half earlier among the Jewish people, and their lives were recorded in the Books of the Maccabees, apocryphal writings from the Old Testament.[4] Seven of them appeared as the so-called seven sons of the widow, and five as the sons of the priest Mattathias who were known as the Maccabees. The seven sons of the widow suffered the most gruesome deaths during the despotic reign of the Syrian king Antiochus Epiphanes, who ruled at the time and against whom the Jews revolted because their faith was threatened with destruction. The five sons of Mattathias took up arms against the powerful king and, with a small but excellent army of courageous fighters, managed to break the superior forces of the Syrians. Judas Maccabeus, hero and victor, established an independent Jewish state with its capital in Jerusalem. He restored the desecrated Temple of Solomon and made it the sacred place of his people again.[5]

The twelve men return to earthly life after a short time, born into the same people and in the same area. Now, however, these souls, who by their shared karma are most deeply connected with the Jewish religion and its Messianic expectations, must find their connection to this divine being in their own personal ways.

In order to perform their service to Christ, they were formed into a higher unity. This was accomplished by the Christ spirit through the use of a mediator, namely the spirit of John the Baptist. Not long after the baptism of Jesus in the Jordan, John was imprisoned and executed by Herod Antipas, the tetrarch of Palestine. His spirit now connected itself with the circle of the twelve as a kind of group-I.

After Lazarus was raised from his mystical death, he joined the twelve. This became possible because the other John, the brother of James, withdrew from the circle. The spirit of John the Baptist worked through the whole group, but especially strongly in the soul of Lazarus-John. We may presume that the new name he received after his initiation was directly related to the spirit of John the Baptist that worked in him.[6]

We are now ready to turn to a consideration of the death and resurrection of Jesus Christ. In what follows, I don't intend to dwell extensively on the events of Holy Week or describe the whole drama of Golgotha. As I see it, the point is to fathom, with the help of spiritual science, what is meant by the death on the cross and the resurrection, what they actually were in reality. Here lies the essential question of Christianity.

9

The Mystery of Golgotha

Those who deny the resurrection, deny Jesus Christ. But what picture does someone who acknowledges the resurrection have of this event? Without spiritual insight based on initiation wisdom we are facing an unfathomable riddle here. Nowhere does the phrase *credo quia absurdum* – I believe because it is absurd – apply so strongly as to the question of Christ's death and resurrection.[1]

We are told that on the day after the Sabbath the women went to the grave of Jesus with balsam herbs and found the stone rolled away and the grave empty. The disciples themselves initially thought that the body of their Lord had been taken by someone and put in another place. But angelic beings told them of Christ's resurrection, and a short time later the disciples saw the Resurrected One 'alive'. However, is the empty grave proof that the body that had been laid there had come back to life, and that Christ showed himself to people the way he had before? Those who believe this cannot have read the gospel texts closely, because these show very clearly that the visible body of the Resurrected One cannot have been the same as the body that had been laid in the grave by Joseph of Arimathea on Good Friday. Would Mary Magdalene, who worshipped and loved Jesus so deeply, not immediately have recognised him after three days? Or the disciples who walked with him on the way to Emmaus? But if the resurrection body differed from the original material body of Jesus, then what did this difference consist of and how can the empty grave be explained?

Before we see what answers spiritual science can give to these questions, we must first consider what preceded the crucifixion on the night of Maundy Thursday.

In the Farewell Discourse in the Gospel of John, which Christ delivers following the Last Supper, Christ speaks of the Father to whom he will go. This teaching about the being of the divine Father is discussed in a lecture Rudolf Steiner gave on the relationship of the Gospel of John to the other gospels.[2] I will summarise this briefly, drawing on what has been discussed earlier in the book about the development of humanity and the period of decline that set in through the Fall and the intervention of Lucifer and Ahriman.

What Christ wanted his disciples to realise is the reality of death, and he called this reality 'the Father'. 'I am going to the Father' means 'I am going into death'. Death is not what human beings believe it to be, the arch-enemy of humanity. That is a fallacy that arose through the workings of Lucifer and Ahriman over the long centuries of decline. Christ came to give to human beings the true being of death; the 'victory over death' must be interpreted as the victory over the false image of death.

Lucifer and Ahriman have placed themselves in front of the Father, obscuring him in order to detach human beings from their origin. Christ did not overcome their influence by destroying them – that is impossible, for they are a part of the plan of creation – but rather by driving them out of Jesus. Human beings can then die in Christ without degenerating. By connecting with Christ, human beings can stand up to the powers of Lucifer and Ahriman. They can continue their development as I-beings in the direction that is shown by the good gods. To the souls that are devoted to him he sends the Comforter, the Holy Spirit, the Spirit of Truth that makes us free. This spirit proceeds from the Father but is sent by the Son who is one with the Father (Jn 15:26).

In the sixteenth chapter, John describes the insecurity felt by some of the disciples as they listen to Christ, who reveals to them the truth and significance of his going, which will plunge them into sorrow:

> Yes, I tell you; you will weep and lament, while other people will be happy. You will be sorrowful, but your grief will be turned into joy (16:20).

He then completed his teaching, which is at the same time an initiation into the secret of his cosmic-earthly mission:

> Yes, I say to you: From now on what you ask from the Father in my name, he will give it to you. Up to now you have not yet prayed in my name. Pray from the heart, and it will be given to your heart, so that your joy may be fulfilled. I have said all this to you in imagery. But the hour is coming when I will no longer speak to you in pictures. Then I will speak openly and plainly to you about the Father. On that day you will pray in my name. I do not say that I will pray the Father for you;

> for the Father himself loves you because you have loved me and have believed that I come from the Father. I went forth from the Father and came into the earthly world; and now I leave the sense-world again and go to the Father. (16:23–28)

The disciples at last understood the profound significance of what had been said to them. They responded:

> 'See, now you are speaking plainly and openly and not in pictures. Now we recognise that everything has been revealed to you. You do not need anyone to question you. And so our hearts confess that you come from the Father.' And Jesus answered: 'Do you now feel my power in your hearts? See, the hour is coming, it has already come, when you all will be scattered, each one into his own loneliness. Then you will also leave me alone; but I am not alone, for the Father is with me. I have said these words to you, so that in me you may find the peace. In the world you have much hardship; but take courage, I have overcome the world.' (16:29–33)

Christ, addressing himself to the Father in heaven, then spoke the High Priestly Prayer, which forms chapter seventeen of the Gospel of John. After that, they left the house where the Last Supper was held, and went to the Garden of Gethsemane on the other side of the Kidron brook.

The final words of the Gospel of John are not to be found in the other three gospels, while the offering of bread and wine as the body and blood of Christ at the Last Supper is not mentioned by John. As in other places in the gospels, this reflects the different viewpoints from which the evangelists give their descriptions. We need to bring these viewpoints together, inwardly, in order to form an image of what reveals itself here as a mystery.

Step by step the initiation – you might also say offering – was enacted through which Christ connected himself more deeply with the circle of the twelve, and connected them with himself. The Passover meal was prepared in a house on Mount Zion. The house belonged to the order of the Essenes and was situated in the place where, in Abraham's time, the sun oracle of Melchizedek was located. Melchizedek was the Priest-King of Salem, a priest of the Most High, who met Abraham (who was then still called Abram) and offered him bread and wine (Gn 14:18).

When the twelve were seated, Jesus got up to wash their feet. The disciples did not understand this gesture at first, and Peter tried to avoid it. But Jesus made it clear to them that this was a ritual act. John describes this washing of the feet as the first step on a Christian path of initiation, which consists in humble gratefulness of the higher order towards the lower one upon which it rests. This gesture of thankfulness and love, which in every spiritual schooling requires the *myste* to develop themselves further in relation to the uninitiated, forms the basis of all true development. No one can lift themselves up without the support of those below them. This was the first deed of offering and it prepared the disciples for the communion that followed.

The Passover meal was a reminder of the first Passover, which took place the night before the exodus from Egypt. A one-year-old lamb was slaughtered and its blood smeared on the door post of every Hebrew home, so that the angel of death, who went around in the night killing all first-born children of the Egyptians, would spare the people of Yahweh (Ex 12:12).

Jesus Christ celebrated for the last time this old Jewish festival, which found its fulfilment in his sacrificial deed. He was the Lamb of God that overcame the power of the angel of death. The eating of the Passover lamb was, in a certain sense, transformed and elevated in the subsequent sacrificial deed.

During the meal, Jesus took the bread and the wine and gave them to his disciples with the words: 'Take, this is my body' and 'This is my blood.'

These words, which are recited during the mass or Eucharist, can only be comprehended by taking them literally. Through his sacrificial deed, which was sealed by his death on the cross, Christ, the cosmic sun spirit, connected himself with the earth. When his blood flowed from the cross into the earth, the sun spirit that was working in this blood permeated the dying substances of the earth and rejuvenated them. The substances of the earth became permeated by his spirit and became the bearers of the Christ spirit. The earth indeed became his body that we tread with our feet when we walk on it. And as the most noble representative of earthly substance, we take the bread that nourishes us. In the sap that rises in earthly plants lives his spirit; it is his blood, just as human blood is the bearer of our 'I'.[3]

From the moment people began to view earthly life and earthly substance merely as dying matter, they could not understand the offering of the Last Supper. Already in the Middle Ages there were disputes about the reality behind it.

Through the sacrament of the Last Supper, human beings

are able to connect themselves with the Christ spirit that works in earthly substance if they are also at the same time able to connect themselves inwardly with Christ. In the lecture he gave on the being of the Father, quoted above, Steiner says: 'Lacking in our hearts the thought that unites us with Christ we cannot engender the force of attraction that draws the Christ Spirit to us at Holy Communion.'[4] And then follow the remarkable words:

> But by means of such a thought form the attraction is generated. For those, then, who need the outer symbol in order to perform the spiritual act – that is, to unite with the Christ – Communion will be the way until such time as their inner strength will have so grown, and they are so permeated by the Christ, that they can dispense with the outer physical agency. The Sacrament of Communion is the preparation for the mystical union with the Christ, the preparatory schooling. That is the light in which we must see these things. And just as everything evolves from matter upward toward spirit under the Christian influence, so those things which existed primarily as a bridge must then grow and develop under the influence of Christ. The Sacrament of Communion must rise from the physical to the spiritual plane if it is to lead to a true union with Christ. One can do no more than hint at such matters, for only if they are received with a full sense of their sacred nature will they be rightly understood.[5]

It is deeply moving that during this most intimate moment of the drama, Judas left the circle to commit his treason: 'So, after receiving the morsel, he immediately went out. And it was night' (Jn 13:30).

The Gospel of John was written out of the direct mystical connection with Christ, which Rudolf Steiner described. The one who wrote it laid his head on the breast of the Master during the Last Supper and received the deepest secrets from his heart. Thus, the contents of chapters fourteen to sixteen should be viewed as the highest expression of this connection, as a true communion.

What then took place in the Garden of Gethsemane below the Mount of Olives is another one of those scenes that in later times has not been understood, because the spiritual sense of the event has been lost. Most people read Jesus Christ's prayer to his Father to 'take this cup from me' as a plea to be spared death, the fear of which he overcomes with the words: 'But not my will, but your will be done' (Lk 22:42). But this is not what the scene in Gethsemane means. Would Christ, a divine cosmic being, really ask to be spared the very thing he had come to earth to accomplish, and which had been prepared over many long ages, simply out of a brief moment of weakness? It flatters our frail humanity to think so, afraid of death as we are, but this fails to take account of how such matters might be viewed by a god. The fear of death that wrung drops of blood from Christ's temples did not take hold of him because he was afraid of dying on the cross, but because he was afraid that he might die too soon.

We must try to imagine how a human being, even one of the highest possible perfection like Jesus of Nazareth, could bear the indwelling presence of the cosmic Godhead for so long. The three years between the baptism and the death on the cross must have been a continuous Passion, a continual burning up of Jesus's body in the fire of Christ's sun spirit. Jesus really was the phoenix that is consumed by fire and rises again from its own ashes.

It was at this moment in the Garden of Gethsemane, just before the arrival of Judas and the soldiers, that the strain of bearing the Christ spirit became almost too much for Jesus of Nazareth. Death threatened, but he could not die yet. Only after suffering torture and being nailed to the cross would Christ completely penetrate even the densest part of his physical body. Without this, some part of material existence would remain forever unredeemed, untransformed by the spirit, and Ahriman would have won.

But the effect of Christ incarnating ever more deeply into Jesus of Nazareth, and the feeling of powerlessness this brought about in him, is what caused the prospect of dying too soon to appear so frightening to him.

Christ had to endure this alone. His disciples had fallen asleep because they were not strong enough to accompany him in consciousness through this deepest trial. With the very greatest effort, Jesus succeeded in overcoming this moment of weakness, this near failure of his task. The entire future of humanity and the world hung in the balance in this lonely struggle amid the olive trees of Gethsemane.

John depicts the events that follow on from this scene as steps on the path of Christian initiation. Beginning with the Washing of the Feet, they continue through the stages of the Scourging and Crowning with Thorns, the Crucifixion and Death and Burial, and finally to the Resurrection and Ascension. Rudolf Steiner spoke in numerous lectures about this Christian-Johannine path of initiation, which he often called the Christian-Gnostic path. It is beyond the scope of this book to go into this path in any more detail.

When Jesus spoke to his disciples about his death and resurrection, he was indicating that what he was about to suffer would take the form of the old initiation. As we know, this consisted of the mystical death of three and a half days after which the initiated one returned to their physical body as though born again, having beheld the secrets of the divine realm. But the initiation that Jesus Christ performed on himself, which he called the lifting up of the Son of Man (Jn 8:28), was of a completely different nature than the ancient mystery initiation. In the latter the human soul was led out of the body upwards into the Kingdom of Heaven. The I was not yet free but was guided by the hierophant. Outside the body, the pupil had spiritual experiences that were preserved in memory after they returned to their earthly body. This enabled the initiated person to act as a messenger of the divine world.

With Jesus Christ it was different. The divine I-being, the cosmic spirit, did depart from Jesus of Nazareth, who therefore died. But Christ returned after three days into the etheric and physical bodies of Jesus, which had been spiritualised by his indwelling and preserved in their spiritual form. In this form Christ was able to show himself to his disciples in such a way that it appeared to them as a visible and tangible physical body.[6]

Hanging on the cross before the eyes of the people, Christ made the old initiation secret visible. The mystical fact had become a historic fact. In this way, however, he also put an end to this ancient initiation and created a new beginning. With the full power of the human I he brought the Kingdom of Heaven into those human beings who are ready to receive it.

These concepts and ideas are among the most difficult to contemplate, and we can only approach them with great reserve and reverence.

Before Christ's incarnation, the human I, the core of the human personality, was so little developed that the forces of the divine realm could not yet penetrate it. If at that time one wanted to gain access to higher worlds, then in a certain sense one had to extinguish one's I. Neither was the human body capable of bearing the indwelling of a fully developed I. Rudolf Steiner speaks about this in another lecture as follows:

> And when all the might of what was later to become the ego and to live within man, when all the power and impulses of the ego filled him, for example through initiation, or through remembering the experience of initiation in a former incarnation in a later one – when the power and might of the ego prematurely penetrated into his bodily nature, what happened then? It has always been pointed out that in the pre-Christian era the ego force, too powerful for the human bodily nature, could not find its proper place in the body, and broke what was destined for the ego. For this reason, those human beings who bear within themselves more of the supersensible world, bearing within themselves in pre-Christian times something of what in a later age would become the ego, such persons split apart their human bodily constitution with this ego force, because this force is too strong for the pre-Christian era.[7]

In myths and sagas this is often expressed by the fact that the initiated ones are vulnerable in one part of their bodies.

For Siegfried it was a spot on his back where a falling linden leaf prevented the dragon blood that made him invulnerable from covering his skin. That was the spot where Hagen's spear pierced him. For Achilles it was his heels because that was where his mother, the sea nymph Thetis, held him when she dipped him in the River Styx to make him invulnerable. Achilles is killed in the Trojan War when an arrow fired by Paris and guided by Apollo strikes him in the heel. Oedipus, who solved the riddle of the Sphinx, was also an initiate. His feet had been pierced and bound together when he was laid as a newborn in the mountains near Thebes to die.

Christ brought the full power of the I to human beings, ushering in this new era in humanity with the words, 'The Kingdom of Heaven is in you.' But what would be the result for the human body if it took this royal power of the I into itself? Such a body would appear to clairvoyant sight as being pierced in five places. The Jewish prophet Zechariah refers to the Christ, the bringer of the I, as the one whom 'they have pierced' (Zec 12:10).

I have already pointed out that the three years that Christ lived and worked in the body of Jesus of Nazareth were a constant suffering, a hidden Passion. You might say that during those years the wounds that became visible on the Crucified One had already been formed by the force of the indwelling of the highest I-spirit in a human body, which pierced this body in five places. The executioners who with rough hammer blows drove the nails through the hands and feet into the wood, and the Roman soldier who pierced Jesus's side with his lance, only outwardly performed what had already happened invisibly: namely, the fivefold piercing of the body by the indwelling of the true I in the human being.

When the blood from these wounds flows onto the earth, it is the beginning of a process that will result in our earth becoming a light-radiating star again, a new sun. The sun that shines now in heaven outside the earth, will in the future be able to unite with the spiritualised Christ-Earth.

Everything we do to hurt or damage the earth we do to Christ.

What then was this resurrection body that the disciples beheld like a physical body, and in which the divine Master appeared before them, spoke with them and ate with them?

If we read the gospel texts carefully it becomes evident that the Resurrected One did not go around in the material body of Jesus, but in a corporeality that must be viewed as something new. But how do we know that this body was not the revived material body of Jesus?

I have already indicated that Mary Magdalene did not initially recognise him, and neither did the two disciples who accompanied him to Emmaus. It is also important that only the disciples saw him and no one else. It was a figure they saw like a physical form, but which was not material. Christ came in through closed doors and vanished from their sight. The disciples experienced his presence, therefore, in brief moments, and we know that this did not last longer than the forty days that led up to Ascension. How do we explain this?

The resurrection body is indeed a physical body, but not a material one. It has a spiritual physicality, but no material density, no weight. The disciples, however, through a dispensation of grace, were able to behold this spiritual, non-material body as if it were tangibly present with them. They were witnesses to the new human being. What occurred in

Jesus through Christ indwelling him for three years was the restoration of the original radiance of the paradisal human being.

We have already discussed how the human being consists of a physical body, an etheric body and an astral body, and how these three bodies form the housing, or the sheaths, of the spiritual core of the human being, the I. Rudolf Steiner's spiritual science describes the evolutionary process that led to the formation of this fourfold human being. In three great cosmic phases that preceded the current planetary incarnation of our earth, beings of the higher hierarchies sacrificed aspects of their own being to create the three lower bodies, forming and transforming them in successive stages.

In the fourth phase, the earth, human beings received the fourth part of their being, the I, again through an outstreaming of divine beings. Those who bestowed the I on human beings at the beginning of earthly development are known in the Old Testament as the Elohim.

In this early stage, which is imaginatively pictured as the Garden of Paradise, the physical body was not yet a material body, it had no mineral content such as it does now. It was a spiritual, archetypal body. In a lecture series Rudolf Steiner gave in 1911 called *From Jesus to Christ,* he refers to this spiritual archetype as the phantom. This phantom, a pure, god-created form, imperceptible to material senses, was the body of the first human being, Adam.[8]

But through the intervention of the Luciferic powers that resulted in the Fall, a counterforce was introduced that not only detached human beings from the higher hierarchies but brought about a total change in them. For the physical body this meant a densification, an absorption of matter, which was accompanied by a deterioration of the original divine body. The latter was, in a certain sense, destroyed. The process of destruction that set in with the Fall is what we call death.

It is important to realise that the physical body allows us to be conscious of our I. It functions like a mirror for our I, and a damaged or broken mirror does not provide a good reflection. As the effects of the Fall spread through human evolution, and the corruptive influence Ahriman was added to that of Lucifer, so the physical body deteriorated and with it the reflection of the I. Human beings risked losing the essence of their being, not knowing anymore who they really were. If this process of deterioration had continued, human beings would in due course have lost their I-consciousness and would no longer be able to develop as a higher spirit.

Christ came to the earth to avert this danger, you might also say, to save the I. In order to restore the physical body to its original, non-material state, he had to make use of a human being who, less than any other, had been affected by the Luciferic-Ahrimanic influence. As we have heard, this human being was the Nathan Jesus, the sister soul of Adam, who had been spared the effects of the Fall, had never incarnated on earth, and who therefore had remained free of all corruptive influences. This being had preserved the power of the phantom in its purest form.

When at his birth in Bethlehem the Nathan Jesus incarnated for the first time in a material body, he of course had to accept the earthly condition of being human, but otherwise he was completely free of the influences of Lucifer and Ahriman. From his twelfth year the Zarathustra I worked in him, preparing him to receive the Christ spirit because Zarathustra, in his many lives on earth, had already connected himself with the macrocosmic sun spirit and could let his wisdom stream into the Nathan Jesus. As we have seen, this preparation was also aided by the spiritual working of the Buddha as the initiate of love and compassion.

After the Zarathustra I departed, the Christ being descended on the thirty-year-old Jesus of Nazareth at the baptism. This prevented what otherwise happens when a normal human I incarnates, namely that the Luciferic-Ahrimanic influence corrupt the phantom and shackle it to the forces of dissolution. The spirit of Christ was able to drive out of the three lower bodies of Jesus of Nazareth whatever had been taken up from Lucifer and Ahriman as a result of taking on an earthly incarnation. After three years, the phantom was already so free of the material corporeality of Jesus that, when he died on the cross, it detached itself from his body like a shining spiritual form.

This is the resurrection body, which for normal eyes was invisible. The disciples, however, were able to perceive it clairvoyantly; it 'densified' before their eyes, even becoming 'tangible' so that doubting Thomas could convince himself of its reality (Jn 20:24–29).

Later on, Paul spoke of the Resurrected One, whom he beheld before the gates of Damascus, as the new Adam, the one who restores the original creative work of the higher hierarchies, the original spiritual body of the human being that was lost with the Fall, to humanity. By the Mystery of Golgotha the seed of a 'new' humanity was sown that will derive its spiritual descent from the resurrection body of Christ, just as the 'old' humanity took its descent from the body of Adam that had become corrupted by the Fall.

10

Ascension and Pentecost

The forty days between Easter and Ascension is mentioned only briefly by the evangelists.[1] The Acts of the Apostles, written by the evangelist Luke who was also a companion of Paul, says of this period:

> By many manifestations of his being [Christ] showed himself as the victor over death after his passion. For forty days he revealed himself to their seeing souls and spoke to them of the mysteries of the Kingdom of God. (Ac 1:3)

Christ told the disciples to remain in Jerusalem and await the one he promised to send them: the Comforter or the Holy Spirit. After they received this Spirit, they became witnesses of Christ 'in Jerusalem and in all Judea and Samaria and to the very end of the earth' (Ac 1:8).

This announcement and directive were followed immediately by the Ascension. We are told that a cloud took Christ up out of sight of the disciples. Two angelic figures then appeared and spoke to the dumbfounded men who stood there looking up:

> This Jesus, who has been taken up before you into heaven, will come again, revealed in the same kind of way as you have now seen him pass into the heavenly sphere. (Ac 1:11)

Here there is a direct reference to what is called the Second Coming of Christ, which is also mentioned in the so-called Little Apocalypse in the twenty-fourth chapter of the Gospel of Matthew. We will discuss this in more detail later, but for now it is worth saying a few words about it.

In the passage quoted from Acts, the Greek word *ouranos* has traditionally been translated as 'heaven' to indicate the place to which Christ ascended. But this has caused misunderstandings throughout the history of Christianity that have had weighty consequences. Since it has been customary to think of *ouranos,* or heaven, as an extraterrestrial realm of divine light far removed from our earthly vale of tears, it has always been assumed that Christ left the earth to dwell with his Father in heaven. He remains receptive to our prayers and rituals, but nevertheless he is far away.

This departure to distant heavenly places is, however, a flagrant contradiction of the words of consolation that appear at the end of Matthew's Gospel: 'And see, I am in your midst all the days until the completion of earthly time' (Mt 28:20).

The problem here is a narrow definition of the word 'heaven'. Christ disappeared from the clairvoyant sight of his disciples in a cloud. But where do we find clouds? They are part of the atmosphere that belongs to the earth. In the description of the ascension in Acts, 'cloud' indicates the etheric world, the sphere of life forces that surrounds and, to a certain extent, also permeates the realm of the elements. Christ did not depart from the earth to heaven; rather, he brought heaven into the sphere of the earth. He became the spirit of the earth by connecting himself with the life of the earth. 'Heaven' is not far away, it is as close as earth. The only difference is that the elemental realm of etheric forces is imperceptible to physical senses. We see the clouds and feel the warmth and the air and the water all around us. We know the sphere of life from the *outside.* Only a clairvoyant can see into the ether world. The disciples were clairvoyant by the grace of Christ's presence and even then only for brief moments. He withdrew this grace in order not to bind them to himself in a manner that would have left them unfree.

Christ came to bring to human beings the full power of the I, and this true I has the divine destiny to develop love on earth. Christ is the master of love, but love can only exist in freedom. The impulse of Christ is, therefore, the impulse of human freedom, and the expression of this is the Holy Spirit that descended on the disciples at Pentecost, ten days after Ascension.

In the previous chapter I mentioned that during the time the disciples were together with Jesus Christ, or were sent out by him into the country, they were in a kind of dream state. This waking dream in which they lived increased towards the end of the great Christ drama. From the moment they accompanied Jesus to the Garden of Gethsemane they fell into a dulled consciousness, which contributed to the fact that, with the exception of John, they were not present at the crucifixion and burial. Peter especially, after denying Christ three times, lapsed into a desperate, darkened state and remained in hiding. It was as if the I of each of them had been torn out of their souls for a time.

Although the disciples had returned to themselves to some extent by Easter morning, in the forty days that followed they were so absorbed by their encounters with Christ in his resurrection body that their powers of comprehension still did not function properly. The I of each of them was not fully present and their experiences still had a dream-like character.

If this condition had continued, the eleven (Judas took his own life after Good Friday) would never have been free in relation to the whole process. This had to be achieved, however, because as the first bearers of the Christ impulse charged with the task of communicating this impulse to the world – not to proclaim his 'doctrine' but to be witnesses of his being – they could do this only as free human beings. In no way could any form of magical influence or dependence on Christ's personal spiritual power determine their apostolic work, even though that same work required them to be filled with the Christ impulse for them to carry it out. How was this achieved?

Christ had overcome the corrupting powers that want to degrade the physical and etheric bodies to the point that human souls can no longer incarnate on earth, and he achieved this for all human beings, even those who do not know Christ or reject him. But if the I and the soul or astral body also want to join the Christ impulse, human beings must find access to this impulse out of their fully awakened individuality. And so that we can tread this conscious, individual path to Christ in freedom, the Holy Spirit is sent.

The Holy Spirit revealed itself on Pentecost morning to the twelve disciples (Judas' place had by then been taken by Matthias). After a rushing sound like the wind in a storm that filled the house, fiery tongues appeared above their heads:

'And they were all filled by the Holy Spirit and began to speak in foreign tongues; each uttered what the Spirit gave him to say' (Ac 2:4).

We must keep in mind that this description given by Luke in Acts is not a sense-perceptible one but a spiritual observation. The tongues of fire that divide and appear above the head of each apostle are no symbolic indications, but an imaginative, spiritually real picture of what happened. In the souls of the apostles themselves this inflow of the Spirit revealed itself in an inspiring way. At that moment, the spirit of humanity spoke through them. We can view the speech Peter then gave to the crowd as a picture of the first proclamation to the world. This became possible because the Pentecost event brought about a mighty awakening in the souls of the disciples.

This awakening occurred in two ways. The individual I of the twelve men, which had in a certain sense been outside them during the previous period, returned just as it does to each human being in the morning after sleep. But at the same time, a higher spiritual being filled all twelve equally. Rudolf Steiner characterises this as follows:

> And with this awakening came a very special feeling. They felt as if something had come to them from the universe which we can only call all-prevailing love. They felt as if they had been quickened by that love coming from above, as if they had been raised from their dream-like state. It was as if all the original power of love that exists in the universe, giving it warmth, had roused them from their sleep, as if this original power of love had entered into the

> soul of each and every one of them. And the people who were able to observe them as they spoke found them completely changed. They knew them to be individuals who had led an extremely simple life until now, though some of them had behaved in a rather strange manner for some days, as if lost in a dream. People had been aware of this. Now, however, they seemed transformed, like individuals who had really and truly entered into a completely new state of mind, a new soul mood. It seemed they had left behind all narrowness and self-seeking and gained infinite greatness of heart, complete inner tolerance and real, heart-felt understanding of all that is human on earth. They were able to express themselves in a way that everyone who was there could understand. People felt that the apostles could see into everyone's heart and soul and read their deepest innermost secrets and were therefore able to comfort every individual, saying exactly what each person needed. It certainly seemed most strange to those observers that a group of people could change in this way.
>
> The individuals who had been transformed, having been aroused by the spirit of cosmic love, now felt a new understanding for events in which their souls had been closely involved but which they had not been able to understand at the time. Now, quickened by cosmic love, understanding dawned in their souls of what had happened on Golgotha.[2]

This is the Holy Spirit: the flaming cosmic power of love that makes everything comprehensible, that places everything in the light of truth, that elevates, expands and transforms the inner being, without forcing it or infringing on its inmost essence. Only love can penetrate the other and ennoble it while leaving it completely free. That which unites all in the spirit does not erase the individual but brings the true fulfilment of human individuality.

The Holy Spirit, as the spirit of love, is the I-spirit of humanity. It is the creative spirit that once hovered over the waters when it emanated from the Father in the beginning, that hovered over the waters of the Jordan as the I-spirit of the Son to incarnate in Jesus of Nazareth. It is the spirit of truth sent by Jesus Christ to awaken consciousness of the Mystery of Golgotha in human souls. It is the Paraclete, the Comforter, who gives unshakable trust in the reality of the resurrection from death.

Through their awakening on Pentecost morning, the disciples were able to look back on the 'dream pictures' of the experiences they had shared with Christ with a new insight. In a prior life, as the sons of the widow and the Maccabees, they had sacrificed themselves for their Messiah. Now he had sacrificed himself for them and for all of humanity by his death on Golgotha. Through the mystery of Pentecost, however, Christ lays into every individual soul the seed that will sprout in the thinking consciousness of the individual human being.

The apostles in their apostle incarnations did again die as martyrs, just as the seed must die in the earth for the plant to grow and flourish. The way of Christ is the way of humanity. It leads through suffering, death, and resurrection to fulfilment by the spirit.

To conclude this chapter, I would like to include the text of the famous medieval hymn to the Holy Spirit, *Veni Creator*

Spiritus:

Come, Holy Ghost, Creator blest,
Vouchsafe within our souls to rest;
Come with Thy grace and heav'nly aid
And fill the hearts which Thou hast made.

To Thee, the Comforter, we cry,
To Thee, the Gift of God Most High,
The Fount of life, the Fire of love,
The soul's Anointing from above.

The sev'n – -fold gifts of grace are Thine,
O Finger of the Hand Divine;
True Promise of the Father Thou,
Who dost the tongue with speech endow.

Thy light to every thought impart
And shed Thy love in every heart;
The weakness of our mortal state
With deathless might invigorate.

Drive far away our wily Foe,
And Thine abiding peace bestow;
If Thou be our protecting Guide,
No evil can our steps betide.

Make Thou to us the Father known;
Teach us the eternal Son to own
And Thee, whose name we ever bless,
Of both the Spirit, to confess.

Praise we the Father and the Son
And Holy Spirit, with them One;
And may the Son on us bestow
The gifts that from the Spirit flow! Amen.[3]

11

Exoteric and Esoteric Christianity

In the development of Christianity in Europe we can distinguish a number of periods. During the first, which lasts for around three hundred years, the apostles and their followers are active spreading the Gospel, and Christianity expands across the whole Roman Empire from East to West. This is also the time of the terrible persecutions by the Roman emperors. In the fourth century Constantine the Great made Christianity a religion of the Roman Empire, and not long after this, Theodosius I made it the official state religion.

In the fourth and fifth centuries important Church Councils were held that established the rules of the faith: the Council of Nicaea in 325, Constantinople in 381, Ephesus in 431, Chalcedon in 451, and Constantinople in 553.

Here we can note three historical developments that had great importance for the progress of Christianity and European culture, and which are still significant today.

The first development related to the outward function of the Church. In a relatively short time the Church as an institution, protected, supported and manipulated by the emperor, became a kind of government apparatus: well organised, disciplined, and invested with power. Christianity was Romanised, meaning that Christian teaching was interpreted as a legal system that focused on guilt (or sin) and forgiveness.[1] It was justice with divine airs. Part of this had to do with the primacy of the Bishop of Rome, the Pope and successor of Peter, who is invested with the power to bind and loose, which is interpreted as the right to condemn or forgive, and the right to impose punishment.

The second development was the growing divide between the Eastern and Western Church, which had made itself felt in several of the early Church Councils. This was centred on the so-called Filioque Controversy: whether the Holy Spirit proceeds only from the Father, as was held to be true in the Eastern Church, or from the Father *and* the Son, as was stated in the Nicene Creed of the Western Church. The debate continued for centuries and, along with other issues, contributed to the Great Schism of 1054. Since that time, Western Roman Catholic Christianity and Eastern Greek Orthodox Christianity have gone their separate ways.

The third development, which is given little attention these days outside of academic circles, consisted of the radical repression and extermination of everything that still had any connection to the ancient mysteries. Not only the expulsion of so-called pagan Greek philosophers and the closing of their centuries-old academies, as well as the systematic wrecking of pagan temples, but also the destruction of scriptures that made a connection between Christianity and the ancient mysteries.

These three developments signify a radical break from original Christianity, which did not vie for external power, and where Roman legalism was still lacking and the connection to the ancient mysteries was still evident. From these developments exoteric Christianity arose – ecclesiastical Christianity, the Christianity of the Church – which had a determining factor in the course of medieval European history.

In modern times a new schism occurred with the Protestant Reformation, which broke from the rigid authority of Rome. But it instituted a strict new authority of its own and no real renewal of the faith. Both for Martin Luther[2] and for John Calvin[3] the theological foundations of the Christianity they preached remained the same as that of the Roman Catholic Church, which was rooted in the work of St Augustine.[4]

If we consider these three developments more closely and try to understand them as more symptomatic of the development of exoteric Christianity, we discover a remarkable paradox. The mandate Christ gave to Peter found its realisation in the creation of a community of people who wanted arrange their lives in such a way that they could devote themselves to following Christ's commands. At the same time, however, anti-Christian forces penetrated the outwardly established Church that manifested itself in this first stage of development.

Although Christ had driven Lucifer and Ahriman out of the bodily sheaths of Jesus of Nazareth, and thereby brought about a source of healing and renewal for all humanity, the forces of evil had not disappeared from the earthly stage. In the early days of Christianity they worked principally through those individuals who wanted to destroy the seedling faith, and to this purpose used terrible cruelty and blind violence. They were not able to infiltrate the ranks of the Christians themselves; the spirit of love and self-sacrifice, the experience of the nearness of the Resurrected One, and the readiness to live like Christ were still too strongly active in those early congregations. When Paul wrote to the early Christian communities, the dangers he warned them about were mostly related to the Luciferic character of atavistic spiritual forces, such as speaking in tongues or somnambulistic prophesying. In those times the most important enemy still came from outside.

When Constantine made Christianity a religion of the Roman Empire, the danger from the enemy now came in the form of vanity, self-satisfaction and the lust for power, especially among the priests. The anti-Christian powers were no less effective in the many theological disputes, which often degenerated into partisanship.

Constantine's decision to recognise Christianity, which was the result of a dream, itself reflects the paradoxical symptoms surrounding the development of the religion. At the time, Constantine was locked in a bitter struggle with his fellow emperor, Maxentius, to become the sole ruler of the Roman Empire. This struggle culminated in the Battle of the Milvian Bridge on the banks of the Tiber in 312. The night before the battle, with Maxentius and his large army securely installed in Rome, Constantine had a dream in which he saw a cross in the sky and the words *In hoc signo vinces* – 'In this sign you will conquer'.

Although Christianity was prohibited in the empire, Constantine ordered his soldiers to paint a cross on their shields and attach a cross to all banners. This was met with tremendous enthusiasm as many of Constantine's Germanic troops were Christians. They marched into battle and defeated Maxentius, who drowned in the Tiber. Maxentius himself had also acted on a dream, in which it was declared that if he left the safety of the city then the enemy of Rome would be destroyed. Spurred on by this, Maxentius rode out to meet the much smaller forces of Constantine in the open field. This proved fateful for him.

To modern, sceptical consciousness this story about dreams is a nice little fable, but from a spiritual point of view it indicates something else, namely the intervention of higher powers in the course of events. It was a spiritual necessity that Christianity assume the more external form subsequently promoted by Constantine, despite the concomitant negative aspects of this. That is how paradoxical history is.

Exoteric Christianity failed to bridge the gap between East and West. The soul life in the Hellenistic part of the empire – those areas that had originally belonged to the empire of Alexander the Great and had a mixture of Greek and Eastern cultural elements – was very different from that which prevailed among the people in the Roman west, whom the Hellenistic people considered barbarians. Indeed, all of Christian culture at the time came from the East. The most important Church Fathers were from the catechumen schools of Alexandria in Egypt and Antioch in Syria, the Church Councils took place in the East, and all scripture, including the gospels and several treatises about the teaching and person of Christ, were Greek.

Slowly but surely, however, the Roman element, with its strong legal and organisational character, began to assume supremacy. Great figures like Tertullian, Ambrose and Augustine began to dominate; Augustine especially became the great authority in matters of faith through his writings. These Western Church Fathers did not write in Greek but in Latin, and, as a consequence, a way of thinking that was inclined towards the abstract displaced the originally living spirituality that is characteristic of the Greek language and Greek thinking.

The Western Roman Empire finally fell apart. Germanic peoples settled in Italy, Spain, Gaul. Then, in 800, Charlemagne, King of the Franks, was crowned Roman Emperor by Pope Leo III. Charlemagne went on to unite most of Western and Central Europe in what became known as the Holy Roman Empire. Western Christendom with the Pope at its head now had an empire as its political foundation again.

During this time the controversy surrounding the Holy Spirit and its relationship to the Father and the Son continued to develop. Personal convictions concerning the Trinity were strongly held, and no one among the ecclesiastical leaders of the Eastern and Western churches possessed either the wisdom or the authority to resolve this question to the satisfaction of both parties.

The matter was further exacerbated by an extremely questionable decision taken during the Eighth Ecumenical Council held in Constantinople in 869, a decision that Eastern Christendom still does not recognise to this day. During this Council the spirit was abolished. Prior to this, the human being was seen as consisting of body, soul and spirit. But now the ruling was adopted that the human being consists only of body and soul, and that the soul has some spiritual aspects. The threefoldness of the human being was eliminated. This brought the anti-Christian powers a lasting victory.[5]

The third development, the destruction of the ancient mystery culture, shows a very determined strategy of both worldly and ecclesiastical figures, who did everything they could to further the outward manifestation of Christianity. They wanted the Church to work as a power apparatus and stripped the Christian faith of everything that had to do with the spiritual wisdom of the ancient mysteries.

According to Rudolf Steiner, this was indeed the deliberate intention of a group of men who have remained largely unknown to history, but who nevertheless exercised an unconscionable influence on ecclesiastical and political life in the transition to the early Middle Ages.[6]

The emperor Julian, who became Roman Emperor shortly after Constantine in the fourth century, and who was viewed with horror by the Church as an apostate and enemy of Christendom, wanted to restore the ancient mysteries and pagan cults. This earned him the enmity of the Church and the name Julian the Apostate.

Julian, who had been initiated into the Eleusinian mysteries, had grown deeply disillusioned with Christianity in its external form and had turned his back on it. He wanted to understand the relationship of Christ to the Sun god of the pagans, but the priests he spoke to were unable to answer his questions. The real enemies of Christianity, the members of the collegium mentioned by Steiner who were instruments of the anti-Christian powers, did not want Christ to be known as the cosmic Sun god who brings the ancient mysteries to fulfilment.

When Julian discovered a Christian stream that knew the secret of Jesus Christ's connection to the sun and perpetuated the ancient mystery wisdom in a Christian way, the collegium ordered his death.[7] Julian was murdered during a military campaign in the Middle East by one of his own troops.

Rudolf Steiner's description of how the Christ was

obscured in this way is deeply moving. He said that after the events in the Holy Land the Christ being went around the still existing ancient mysteries to renew them. But through the systematic destruction of these mysteries, however, he underwent a second crucifixion:

> However, just as the first Mystery of Golgotha took place in Palestine, so was the second enacted by the impulse brought by Constantine; for the eradicating of the mysteries led to Christ, as a historical reality, being crucified, killed for a second time. The terrible destruction that spread over several centuries was not merely a destruction of artistic and mystic treasures (though this should not be underestimated) but the destruction of vast swathes of human experience. But there was no understanding of what had actually been destroyed and had disappeared, because any real depth of understanding had been lost.[8]

Concurrent with the development of exoteric Christianity, there evolved another, more esoteric stream, which also ran principally from east to west. This stream remained hidden in the background of events. It did not strive for outward visibility as ecclesiastical Christianity had done, but for a deeper, more inward approach to the Christ mystery. We might call this stream the path of Christian initiation; it is also called Johannine Christianity or Grail Christianity.

It is hidden partly because historians have tended to focus too much on exoteric Christianity to follow the traces of this esoteric tradition, but also because this stream is indeed about hidden things. It is about a search for a direct and personal connection with the being of Christ that is achieved not through the rituals of the Church, but by following a path of initiation. Very little of this has ever appeared openly on the stage of world history, though occasionally we have had glimpses of it, such as in the persecution of the Cathars in the south of France and the destruction of the Knights Templar in the twelfth and thirteenth centuries.

Although we can regard this esoteric Christianity as one stream, there are nevertheless a number of strands within it connected with the direct disciples of Christ.[9] Despite the many statements by Rudolf Steiner and the extensive literature that exists about its legendary aspects (especially concerning the Grail tradition), this esoteric stream still presents us with riddles that need to be investigated and fathomed. I will mention only a few main points here and focus on individuals from whom certain streams within the general esoteric movement have proceeded.

In the first place, there is the figure of John, the inaugurator of a Christian path of initiation. John, who as Lazarus was initiated by Christ himself, indicates in his gospel the way to Christ. In the sevenfold path of the stages of the Passion – the Washing of the Feet, Scourging, Crowning with Thorns, Crucifixion, Death, Burial, and Resurrection – the soul is gradually purified and the Virgin Sophia is developed in one's own being. This enables the higher self, the Holy Spirit principle, which is connected with Christ, to be born in the individual human being.

Rudolf Steiner called this the Johannine-Gnostic way and although it aimed at a meditative deepening of feelings through the seven stages, it was still a way of achieving knowledge or gnosis. During the schooling of their consciousness on the

Johannine path, the aspirant crossed the threshold to the spiritual world and came to know the secrets of the cosmos and the human being. This form of initiation, for which Christ himself was the hierophant, demanded complete dedication from the aspirant to the prescribed meditative exercises. They had to withdraw completely from social life, in most cases for a considerable time, to practice the exercises in total seclusion.

John connected his path of initiation with what had lived in pre-Christian times in the mysteries of Ephesus on the west coast of Asia Minor. Through initiation into these moon mysteries the aspirant was brought into a relationship with the creative Word of Worlds, the Logos. John identified Christ with the Logos, and thus his esoteric path is a Christianisation of the Virgin Mother mystery path of the ancients. Another path that led to the Word of Worlds was the Egyptian Isis initiation.[10] This initiation, however, led the aspirant into the depths of their soul, whereas in the Ephesian mysteries the pupil was led out into the cosmos.[11]

A second strand within Christian esotericism comes from Paul, the apostle to the gentiles. Paul, also called Saul, was a Jewish initiate who came from Tarsus, a city on the south coast of Asia Minor that had a flourishing, Hellenistic culture. Paul must have been thoroughly familiar with Stoic philosophy, which was also a Logos philosophy. As a Pharisee, who therefore had very definite opinions about the Messiah, Paul as Saul strongly opposed the men from Galilee who regarded their rabbi as the Messiah. Paul proceeded to persecute the followers of Jesus Christ in Jerusalem and beyond. But on his way to Damascus he had a vision of the resurrected Christ. From that moment, he knew that the people he had so fiercely pursued were right: Jesus was the Messiah. Paul became a follower of Christ, which for him meant taking Christ into his soul. His initiation – for that is what his experience outside Damascus really was – allowed him to perceive the Christ in his etheric light form in the aura of the earth. This is a future condition for the rest of humanity, but one that Paul received as an act of grace.

Paul later founded a Christian mystery school in Athens, close to the important mystery site of Eleusis. Paul had visited Athens some years before and had spoken to the members of the Areopagus assembly. Among them was a man later known as Dionysius the Areopagite, an initiate of Eleusis who had had a supersensory vision of the Mystery of Golgotha. When he heard Paul speak he recognised in Paul's words what he had himself experienced. Paul now chose the older man to lead his school.[12]

The esoteric teachings given in this school, which just as in the old mystery schools were communicated orally, were concerned with the Christianisation of the old mystery wisdom surrounding the divine hierarchies, the inhabitants of the heavenly realms. Sometime in the late fourth or early fifth century, part of these teachings were written down. The author, who also called himself Dionysius, was initially considered to be the same as the original leader of the Athens school. Later language scholars discovered that this could not be correct, however, because the book on the heavenly hierarchies was written in a much later form of Greek than the language of the first century, when Paul's friend and disciple had lived.

The doctrine of the heavenly hierarchies was subsequently brought into disrepute because it was said that the document was counterfeit. The author himself was referred to as Pseudo-Dionysius. But that fails to grasp that leaders of esoteric schools always used the name of their first master. The later Dionysius did not counterfeit anything, he only wrote down what until then had been passed on from mouth to ear.

The doctrine of the celestial hierarchies with its esoteric content has played a significant role in exoteric Christianity. We only need think of angelic statues in cathedrals and graveyards or of Thomas Aquinas's work on the angels. Eventually, however, the intellectualism of modern times, together with the rise of materialism, has robbed the Christian culture of these riches. Protestantism especially has contributed to the 'depopulation' of heaven and turned Christianity into the most barren and abstract monotheism imaginable.

It is interesting that the legend of Saint Denis (who was also called Dionysius), which is described in *The Golden Legend*, a collection of stories about the lives of the saints written by the thirteenth century Italian chronicler Jacobus de Voragine, lets Dionysius, the Greek friend of Paul, travel to Western Europe and die a martyr's death there. The historical basis of this story is not easy to find. His work on the hierarchies – or rather, of his later successor who wrote it down – did indeed go to the West. It was translated into Latin in the ninth century by the Irish monk John Scotus Eriugena,[13] who worked at the court of Charles the Bald, King of the Franks.[14] Many of the Irish monks still knew Greek (unlike the more Rome-oriented Benedictines), and Irish or Celtic Christianity, which played an important role in Europe in the sixth, seventh, and eighth centuries, was still filled with cosmic wisdom. In a certain respect it can be considered part of the esoteric Christian stream.

A third strand of esoteric Christianity is represented by the figure of Joseph of Arimathea, in whose family tomb the body of Christ was laid, and has to do with the legend of the Holy Grail. According to the twelfth-century French poet Robert de Boron, Joseph of Arimathea caught the blood that flowed from Christ's wounds in the cup that was used in the Last Supper.[15] From this vessel Jesus gave the wine to his disciples with the words, 'Drink, this is my blood.' In the Grail tradition the Holy Grail itself is not so much a real wine vessel but a symbol of the incarnation of Christ. Of course, this does not preclude that there may really have been such a wine vessel.

According to the legend, Joseph of Arimathea was imprisoned by the Jews, but with the destruction of Jerusalem in the year 70 he was freed by Vespasian, who commanded the Roman troops in Palestine and became emperor. The Grail, which the Resurrected One had brought to Joseph in his dungeon, had nourished and kept him alive all those years. With a small group of family members, he travelled to England where he landed in the southwest near Glastonbury. This is where the connection is made between the Grail and the legends of King Arthur and the Knights of the Round Table. This was an initiation community that was inspired by ancient Irish-Hibernian mysteries.[16] Just like the apostles John and Paul, Joseph of Arimathea was looking for a connection with one of the most important pre-Christian mystery centres, in this case in Western Europe. Esoteric Christianity did not cut the ties with ancient mystery wisdom, as Roman exoteric Christianity did, but tried to make a connection with the old, so that this could come to fulfilment and renew itself in the Christian stream. The story of Parsifal that emerges from this refers to the Grail stream in the ninth century. Here, too, the court of King Arthur and its connection to Celtic esotericism plays an important part.

I also want to mention an extremely important stream in esoteric Christianity that initially moved more to the East, far into China and Mongolia, but also left distinct traces in Europe. I am referring to the stream of Manichaeism, which was founded by the great initiate Mani or Manes in the third century. According to Rudolf Steiner's research, the founder of this mighty Christian-Gnostic movement had been a follower of Jesus Christ in a previous life. In Mani we see the reborn youth of Nain mentioned in Luke's gospel who was raised from the dead by Christ.

Manichaeism was fiercely opposed by the Roman Church, especially by Augustine. It was practically eradicated in Europe, and persecuted in Asia by the rulers of the Sassanid Empire.[17] It lasted for a long time in the East but was eventually overcome by Genghis Khan and other conquerors.[18] In recent times, Manichaeism has been receiving a lot of attention again from theologians, scientists and interested laymen.

Esoteric Christianity found a certain continuation in the streams of the Cathars and the Knights Templars, both destroyed by Rome, and finally in the Rosicrucian movement. At the beginning of the seventeenth century this movement came to popular attention with the publication in 1615 of a few, supposedly esoteric documents, the best known of which are *The Chemical Wedding of Christian Rosenkreutz* and *Fama Fraternitatis,* both by Johann Valentin Andreae.

In the European countries where Protestantism had spread, we clearly see an influence of this esoteric Christian brotherhood. It had a distinct influence on statesmen, scientists, mystics and artists, the best known of which are Shakespeare, Rembrandt, Jakob Böhme and Johann Sebastian Bach. It also very clearly worked in the German poet Johann

Goethe and some of his contemporaries. The Freemasons also absorbed much from the original Rosicrucians.[19] In the eighteenth century this stream concentrates itself in the mysterious and misunderstood figure of the Count of St Germain, whose influence in politics was considerable.

In the nineteenth century Christian esotericism petered out, then, at the beginning of the twentieth century, Rudolf Steiner picked up the thread again. With anthroposophy he created a modern Christian initiation movement that was as much a metamorphosis and renewal of the original stream as it was a continuation.[20]

12

Reincarnation and Karma

In the last three chapters of this book, I will look at three themes that are of great importance to a new vision of Christianity based on spiritual research. I will start with a few words on reincarnation and karma and their relationship to Christianity.

Neither the Roman Catholic nor the Protestant churches accept the reality of reincarnation. In my opinion, that is based on a misunderstanding, albeit an understandable one. It is true that Christian doctrine, to the extent that it can be distilled from the gospels and the other books of the New Testament, does not include teaching on reincarnation. On the other hand, it is not difficult to demonstrate that at the time of Christ's incarnation, knowledge about reincarnation still lived in people everywhere. We can find clear indications in the gospels that reincarnation was not considered an unusual or unacceptable idea. I have already pointed to the statement about John the Baptist being the reborn prophet Elijah, and it was mentioned in the discussion Christ had with his disciples about the healing of the man born blind. In the spiritual-scientific contemplations developed in this book, reincarnation and karma have come up repeatedly.

A critical mind might object that this interpretation has been imposed from outside; it cannot be deduced from any of the texts themselves. But the rejection of reincarnation and karma by mainstream Christianity is not based on the belief that they do not form part of Christian teaching. Rather, because people think of karma as allowing for the atonement of sins over successive lifetimes, they think this invalidates Christ's redemptive sacrifice. That kind of 'self-redemption' is rejected as un-Christian.

As so often happens, people who hold these opinions are fighting notions they have first fabricated themselves. The view that Christian redemption and the law of karma are mutually exclusive is a misconception, and one that can be thoroughly refuted by a study of Rudolf Steiner's work.

Christ did not incarnate on earth to free people from their guilt. That would deny us the opportunity to set right what we have done wrong and thereby take full responsibility for ourselves and our actions, which is what it means to be a free human being. That is karma. What then is the burden of sin that Christ takes onto himself? What does he free us from? Christ takes onto himself that part of our guilt that we cannot settle through our karma.

In all that we do wrong, whether out of ignorance, egoism or lovelessness, and all that we neglect to do, those sins of omissions, there are two aspects. One is a subjective aspect, what we do to ourselves and others. When we hurt someone, we also diminish our own dignity. This is the part we must compensate for in subsequent lives.

But another part consists of the objective damage we cause to the world as a whole. All our lovelessness, antipathy, egoism and deliberate malignance inflicts damage on the perfection of the world order. It inflicts lasting damage on the divine structure of the universe. It is a disharmony in the world symphony. This is objective evil, a lasting interference, and we are incapable of setting it right or restoring it. Only the highest creative being himself can do this by taking the evil into himself.

Christ relieves us and the world of the objective evil that is continually committed due to our deficiencies. He is the Lamb that bears the burden of sins of the world.[1] If he did not do this, the damage thus inflicted on the world would degrade the divine order to the point that no life, no soul, no spirit would be able to exist in it anymore.

In the chapter on the 'I AM' sayings of Christ in the Gospel of John, we have already mentioned the woman who was caught in adultery and brought before Christ by the scribes and Pharisees (Jn 8:3–11). According to the Law of Moses, the penalty for adultery is death by stoning.[2] The scribes were trying to trick Jesus into speaking against the Law, knowing that he, compassionate and loving, would probably plead to let the woman live. Jesus Christ, however, responded to this trap in a way that is significant for the future development of humanity.

The scribes said to him: 'Master, this woman has been caught in the act of adultery. In the Law, Moses commands us to stone such women. What do you say about it?' To begin with, Christ gave no answer. He bent down and wrote with his finger in the earth. The scribes and the Pharisees didn't realise that he was calling their attention to karma: the guilt of the woman is written in the earth. The Pharisees repeated their question, but Christ did not fall into their trap and speak against the Law. Instead he said: 'Whoever among you is free of sin, let him throw the first stone at her.' Again, he bent down and wrote in the earth. The woman's accusers quietly departed, one at a time, the oldest first. Jesus was left with the woman and asked her where her accusers had gone and whether anyone had condemned her. She replied: 'No one, Lord.' Jesus then said to her: 'I do not condemn you either. Go, and from now on do not sin anymore.'

Twice, therefore, Christ pointed to karma by writing in the earth. In a subsequent life on earth, the woman will have to take on the consequences of her deed and compensate for it. The subjective part of her guilt is then paid off. The objective aspect is not directly mentioned, but with the words 'I do not condemn you either', Jesus indicated that he takes this aspect on himself. He was the one who might have thrown the first stone, for he was without guilt. He changed the penalty from the implacable Law into an appeal to the freedom of the woman: 'From now on do not sin anymore.' She can overcome the temptation to sin out of the forces of her own free I. It was an appeal to her conscience.

This deeply moving scene demonstrates that guilt and punishment or forgiveness will appear in a different light when humanity recognises the reality of karma and freedom and lives accordingly. Before Christ, karma was retribution according to the Law. Adultery is punished with death by stoning. Moses stands as the stern judge in God's name on the threshold of the spiritual world. Many people continue to live in this belief: God punishes sin, God is just. He gave the Law of his divine retribution and justice to Moses for humanity. Christ does not speak against this Law, but takes away the revenge, the retribution, with his love. He takes karma into his being and becomes the Lord of Karma.

Human society will be transformed when people realise the reality of karma and how it leads to freedom through the working of our conscience. This realisation is the reality of the new Christ experience.

When people are unable to accept the idea of karma and reincarnation as deeply Christian, they are incapable of viewing their own karmic experiences in the light of the ongoing development of humanity. For this is the development from unfreedom to freedom, from the Law of Moses to the love of Christ.

For two thousand years, ecclesiastical Christianity has kept the door closed to reincarnation and karma. Anyone who believed in these ideas were either persecuted or ridiculed. And yet there have been many representatives of Western culture who have accepted them and found them to be fruitful ideas, including Gotthold Lessing, Johann Goethe, William Blake, Richard Wagner and many others.

The world is changing, and reincarnation and karma are no longer rejected as ridiculous or condemned as un-Christian. We can sense the very first beginnings of a new Christianity, in which these ideas are viewed as profoundly Christian truths, and where efforts are made to live according to them.

13

The Second Coming

After the foregoing discussion on reincarnation and karma, some people might be inclined to think that Jesus Christ himself is subject to repeated earthly lives and might reincarnate to renew his teaching. There are indeed people who have thought this, and there are surely others who still do, in part because the Gospel of John and the Book of Revelation speak of a second coming.

However, a second coming in the sense of a re-embodiment in a physical body is out of the question. The Mystery of Golgotha, which led to the forming of the resurrection body, cannot be repeated in the material world. Whoever believes in a physical second coming has not understood the death and resurrection of Jesus Christ in its unique essence. Those who think or expect that Christ will come back to the earth view Christianity primarily as a doctrine and not as a deed. A teacher can renew his teaching in a subsequent incarnation, but a sacrificial deed of the highest Godhead, as was performed on Golgotha, can take place only once.

At the beginning of the twentieth century, an Indian boy named Jiddu Krishnamurti was proclaimed by the Theosophical Society as the next incarnation of Christ, and an organisation, the Star of the East, was set up with the young

Krishnamurti at its head.[1] Rudolf Steiner, then the head of the German Section of the Theosophical Society, saw this as a profound misunderstanding of the Mystery of Golgotha and eventually broke with the society.

From 1910, when this conflict was taking place, Steiner gave a large number of lectures on the appearance of Christ in the etheric world.[2] In these lectures he referred to a second coming not 'in the flesh', not in a material body, but in the etheric figure of light that Paul had beheld outside Damascus. According to Steiner, this phenomenon would begin around the year 1933. He said that only a few people would experience the etheric Christ at first, but that this number would increase in the future. It means that in our time a new clairvoyance will grow in humanity, of which the first seed is laid by such a meeting with Christ.

It is evident that this Damascus experience is a very personal matter, and it is in no way confined to people who call themselves Christians. Steiner described how people who experience difficult times will suddenly feel the presence of the etheric Christ as a consolation:

> For we have now reached the point of time when the etheric Christ enters into the life of the earth and will become visible – at first to a small number of individuals through a form of natural clairvoyance. Then in the course of the next three thousand years, he will become visible to greater and greater numbers of people. This will inevitably come to pass in the natural course of evolution. That it will come to pass is as true as were the achievements involving electricity in the nineteenth century. A number of individuals will see

> the etheric Christ and will themselves experience the event that took place at Damascus. But this will depend upon such people learning to be alert to the moment when Christ draws near to them. In only a few decades from now it will happen … that some individual here or there has certain experiences. If he has sharpened his vision through studying anthroposophy, he may become aware that suddenly someone has come near to help him, to make him alert to this or that. The truth is that Christ has come to him, although he believes that what he saw was a physical human being. He will come to realise that what he saw was a supersensible being, because it immediately vanishes. Many a person will have this experience when sitting silent in his room, heavy-hearted and oppressed, not knowing which way to turn. The door will open, and the etheric Christ will appear and speak words of consolation to him. The Christ will become a living comforter to human beings. However strange it may as yet seem, it is true nevertheless that many a time when people – even in considerable numbers – are sitting together, not knowing what to do, and waiting, they will see the etheric Christ. He will himself be there, will confer with them, will make his voice heard in such gatherings. These times are approaching, and the positive, constructive aspect now described will take real effect in the evolution of mankind.[3]

I would not have included this long quotation if it weren't indeed possible to mention experiences that correspond with what Steiner here predicted. Indeed, we find a similar scene described in the semi-autobiographical fragment that appears in the prologue to the French philosopher Simone Weil's book *La connaissance surnaturelle* [Supernatural knowledge]. In it she describes how someone once came to her as she sat alone in her attic, spoke with her and ate bread with her. He took her to a church and said that she should pray, and then left her rather abruptly. She writes at the end:

> I know very well that he does not love me. How could he love me? And yet, deep in me there is something, a piece of myself, that cannot refrain from thinking, trembling with fear, that perhaps, despite everything, he yet loves me.[4]

It is a heartrending testimony from a young woman who was so badly treated by life that she did not dare believe that her mysterious visitor loved her.

In his lectures on the reappearance of Christ, Rudolf Steiner explained that following the end of the Kali Yuga[5] in 1899, a five-thousand-year period in which the god-forsakenness of humanity reached its deepest point, a new age of light began. Etheric clairvoyance, which in the distant past was a natural human capacity before the development of reflexive thinking and sharp sensory perception, will arise again in a new and fully self-conscious way. The etheric body will loosen itself from the physical body into which it sank ever more deeply over the course of time, which is what led to the disappearance of the old clairvoyance.

Indeed, in our time we are seeing all kinds of supersensory experiences occurring in people. The explanation of this is the loosening of the etheric body. There is a danger, however, that the new clairvoyant capacity, which we may view as a gift from Christ, will fall into the grip of anti-Christian powers. It is their intention to corrupt this spiritual gift so badly that it becomes unworkable or won't be recognised for what it is, either being considered a spiritual abnormality or some kind of psychiatric condition.

That is why it is of such great importance to be prepared for these coming events by spiritual science. Steiner expressed this very clearly on many occasions: anthroposophy had to come into the world in order to prepare people for the reappearance of Christ in the etheric, the most important event in our time.

As I mentioned in an earlier chapter, demonic beings recognise Christ before human beings do. That is also the way it is in our time. The demonic attack perpetrated on humanity by the Nazis under Adolf Hitler was without doubt directed against this new revelation of Christ. The year 1933, which Rudolf Steiner mentioned on different occasions as the beginning of the etheric appearance of Christ, began with Hitler becoming Chancellor of Germany. Millions of souls, especially those of young people, were subsequently dimmed by the fervour that gripped the nation and were therefore cut off from the possibility of experiencing the Second Coming. The regime, which worked in service of the Antichrist, who can be viewed as the direct inspirer of Hitler, eventually banned the Anthroposophy Society, which wanted to point to the etheric Christ.

This brings us to the last subject to be discussed in this connection, namely the Apocalypse or the Revelation of John, which has particular relevance for our times. The revelation of Christ, which is what this book is about, is at the same time a revelation of the Antichrist, the counterforce that opposes humanity as it attempts to spiritualise its consciousness and puts humanity to the ultimate test. Coming to our aid, however, is the great guardian of the spiritual realm, the servant of Christ and the angel of the apocalypse: Michael.

14

The Apocalypse

If I wanted to present the Apocalypse, the Book of Revelation, in a satisfactory manner, it would require an entire book itself. In this chapter I can only mention a few key points.[1]

The Apocalypse, which John dictated to his companion during his exile on the Greek island of Patmos, gives us awesome visionary pictures of the end of the world.[2] The strange and often frightening imagery in this book has exercised a strong hold over the cultural imagination in the two thousand years since it was written. This is especially true of the scene of the Last Judgment, in which the wicked are separated out from the good and condemned to eternal damnation. In the Requiem, the Catholic mass held for the dead, this is the *Dies irae* – the day of wrath. The rest of the book has not played such a large role in the faith, in spite of the marvellous representations of it in miniatures and paintings, and in the form of sublime tapestries. A few great spirits in the Middle Ages occupied themselves intensively with the Apocalypse, such as the Calabrian abbot and mystic Joachim of Fiore[3] and the Italian poet Dante Alighieri.[4]

Theologians and laymen of later times lacked the spiritual comprehension necessary for understanding this book, let alone for finding any Christian consolation in it. Martin Luther did not want to make it part of his translation of the Bible because he was unable to discover the Christ of the gospels in it.

Our time has adopted a strongly apocalyptic character – in this context meaning ruin and destruction – with its emphasis on nuclear war, holocaust, genocide and environmental degradation. As a result, interest in the last book of the Bible has increased among religious circles. But our usual, materialistic thinking is even less able to understand this book than it is the gospels. If there is one book we may justifiably call a book of initiation, it is the Revelation to John. In order to offer some explanation of the esoteric pictures contained in this book, I will once again draw on the spiritual science of Rudolf Steiner.

After a prologue in which Christ appears as the archetype of the human being, as the cosmic Son of Man, the reader – or rather the beholder or hearer – is led through a series of phases or conditions which, in their sevenfoldness, increase in dramatic tension towards the climax of the narrative. By the end, not only the earth but the entire cosmic order have been completely transformed.

These sequences of seven phases each must be regarded as long eras in the future development of the earth, which also represent at the same time successive levels of higher forms of consciousness. As has been stated before, the number seven points to development in time. The alchemical process of recasting is a process of spiritualisation. Everything that descended into dense materiality must in the future be transformed into a higher, non-material form of being. This ultimately appears in the picture of the New Jerusalem, the 'new' earth.

The seer and initiate John was able to follow this process in an out-of-body state. What he therefore described is both a path of initiation for individuals and the drama of earthly creation. The three higher forms of consciousness I have mentioned before, imagination, inspiration and intuition, are marked by three sevenfold phases: the seven seals (imagination), the seven trumpets (inspiration), and the seven bowls of wrath (intuition). Regarding the last phase, I prefer the translation used by Jon Madsen, who for the Greek word *thumos,* which is usually translated as 'anger' or 'wrath', uses instead 'divine will'. This avoids the association of wrath with retribution and revenge.

Another phase of seven precedes the ones mentioned above, namely the letters to the seven congregations in Asia Minor. These congregations, which really existed at the time when John received his revelation, are to be viewed here as pictures of the seven cultural epochs that in anthroposophical spiritual science are called the seven post-Atlantean cultures. Each letter corresponds with an epoch of a little over two thousand one hundred years, beginning with the first cultural epoch in India around 7000 BC. Our present epoch, which began in AD 1413, is the fifth of the seven and corresponds with the fifth letter, which is addressed to the congregation in Sardis.

In the fourth chapter, between the seven letters to the congregations in Asia Minor and the opening of the seven seals, we find a mighty spiritual vision of the heavenly world. A throne appears on which the high divine being is seated, who is here not mentioned by name. In his hand he holds a scroll that is closed with seven seals. Around him are the four animals with whom the four evangelists are associated, as we heard in the chapter on the gospels. These winged animals represent the sphere of the cherubim, which finds its expression in the zodiac (the word 'zodiac' comes from the Ancient Greek meaning 'circle of little animals'). They are the spirits of harmony, the high ordering principle that shines out from the Creator.

Also around the heavenly throne are twenty-four elders, crowned figures who hold musical instruments in their hands. In a later chapter of Revelation we will hear that these mysterious elders sing a 'new song' (Rv 5:9). They are, according to Rudolf Steiner's spiritual interpretation of the Apocalypse, the representatives of the epochs that have preceded the current moment in cosmic development.

In this lofty, initially static image of eternity, a very great tension arises when an angel asks who is worthy to undo the seals of the book. At first no one takes up the call to open the book and read from it; no one is able to inaugurate a new phase of development. It is as if the creation comes to a halt, and John weeps because no one proves worthy to do this. But then one of the Elders speaks and says: 'Do not weep! See. The lion of the tribe of Judah, the Root of David, has won the victory. He can open the book and its seven seals.' And before the throne and in the midst of the winged animals and the Elders, John sees a lamb standing 'as though it had already been slain' (Rv 5:5–6).

The sacrificial lamb, Jesus Christ, the son of David raised up by the Christ spirit, brings movement, progress and therefore fulfilment to the stagnating world of the old creation.

From that moment, the future unfolds with the opening of the seals, the sounding of the trumpets, and finally the pouring out of the divine bowls. During this process of transformation a crisis occurs. Crisis means 'judgment' but also 'separation', in this case separation of those who want to go with Christ from those who don't.

John, the human being who was initiated by Christ himself, witnesses this process, but not as a spectator who only watches from outside, but as one who is personally engaged. Whoever accompanies him in this development discovers that from the divine-spiritual world there is a helping power at work that guides humanity through these events. This power is an angelic being with an exceptional divine mandate. He is initially not mentioned by name, but we later come to know it in the twelfth chapter: Michael, the archangel of the sun, the messenger of Christ. We might also call him the archangel of humanity.

He appears even before he is mentioned by name as the opponent of the dragon or Antichrist in a scene that is of special significance for our time. For although the Apocalypse mostly shows future events in visionary pictures, we must realise that the future works in advance just as the past has its aftereffects, and what is taking place now is a foreshadowing of later phases. In the tenth chapter John stands at a threshold, and a mighty being descends from heaven in front of him:

> And I saw another angel of great strength; he descended from heaven, clothed in a cloud. About his head the rainbow shone, his face was like the sun and his feet were like pillars of fire. In his hand he held a small open book. He placed his right foot on the sea, the left on firm ground. And he called out with a great voice which was like the roar of a lion. (Rv 10:1–3)

This figure can be viewed as a heavenly guardian who appears before every human being as they are about to pass from earthly to super-earthly consciousness. The guardian's pillar-like feet form the threshold of this transition. In a later phase, Lucifer and Ahriman will appear where this being has placed his feet as the beast that rises from the sea and the beast that rises from the land. Every human being, all of humanity therefore, comes to this threshold or gateway of the spiritual realm and is confronted with the powers of evil.

Our time can only be understood as a foreshadowing of this threshold experience. All the trials humanity is currently undergoing – the increasing mechanisation of society, the growing sensuousness of physical existence, the awful suffering of millions of people, and, by contrast, the scandalous ways in which those in positions of wealth and power try to ignore the unavoidable breakthrough of the apocalyptic crisis – all of this is a foreshadowing of what John beholds as a future process.

The future is already here. With the ending of Kali Yuga, time grows ever more urgent. In the Apocalypse it has gone into intense acceleration.

Then, in the twelfth chapter, we get the real message of the Book of Revelation. The seer beholds the picture of a heavenly woman who is in the pains of childbirth. She is crowned with stars and clothed with the sun, and she has the moon under her feet. Before her stands a great fiery red dragon with seven heads and ten horns. On each head the dragon wears a diadem. The dragon wants to devour the woman's child, but when the child is born – 'a son; he shall shepherd all peoples with an iron staff' – he is snatched away and 'caught up to God and his throne. And the woman fled into the desert ...

There she is to eke out her existence for twelve hundred and sixty days.' (Rv 12:1–6)

This heavenly woman, the Mary-Sophia being in its cosmic manifestation, is the essence of the human soul. Out of the soul the spirit child, the higher I, is born. The iron staff indicates the connection with the I.[5] The higher I of the human being is still 'with God'; it can only fully reveal itself once it has absorbed the Christ power. The power of the Antichrist, the dragon, opposes this. The dragon cannot 'devour' the higher, spiritual human being, and thus it turns its rage against the soul, the 'heavenly woman' in us. All warfare between good and evil, light and darkness, is a struggle for the soul. The Apocalypse expresses the outcome of this struggle in a double image: the heavenly city of Jerusalem as opposed to the earthly city of Babylon, which is destroyed. Another contrasting pair of images shows the bride who joins the heavenly bridegroom, the lamb, and the whore of Babylon who joins the Beast. The latter is the soul that cannot let go of matter and has become ensnared in power and sensuality, blind to the loving sacrificial deed of Christ.

The appearance of the dragon sparks a mighty conflict in heaven, with Michael, the great champion of human freedom, leading the charge against him:

> And a war flared up in the heavenly world. Michael and his angels fought against the dragon. And the dragon fought in the midst of his angels. But his strength failed, and so there was no longer a place for them in the heavens. The great dragon was overthrown, the primeval serpent who is of both diabolic and satanic nature, the Tempter of all mankind. (Rv 12:7–9)

In the thirteenth chapter, the two powers of evil, which at first were united in the form of the dragon, now appear separately as the beast that rises from the sea and the beast that rises from the land. The second beast appears in the form of a lamb with two horns, which indicate that its manifestation as a lamb is an illusion: this being is the Antichrist who, by assuming the appearance of innocence and goodness, seduces human beings and destroys them. He possesses great power, and those who cannot resist his magical temptations receive a mark from him on the right hand and on the forehead, and he makes it impossible for anyone, except he who bears the mark, to buy or sell (Rv 13:16–17). This shows that this power works through the economy, and as such this anti-Christian power is extremely active and evident in our time.

This second beast is then described with the mysterious number 666. This number can be understood in several ways. The first is as an occult number that refers to different stages in earth evolution: 6 – 6 – 6. If we were to express our current time in a similar occult way, the number would be 4 – 4 – 4. The first number refers to the earth as the fourth cosmic-planetary phase in the development of our solar system, which was preceded by three other planetary conditions, known in anthroposophy as Old Saturn, Old Sun and Old Moon. This earth phase can then be subdivided into seven conditions of life, which are themselves divided into seven conditions of form. We are in the fourth condition of life, the mineral kingdom, and in the fourth condition of form, the physical-etheric state, hence the number 4 – 4 – 4. (There are further subdivisions of these great rounds that relate to great epochs and cultural epochs, but they don't concern our immediate considerations here.) The number 6 – 6 – 6 therefore relates to a far distant future, just before the start of the seventh and last cosmic-planetary phase known in anthroposophy as Vulcan, when the choice humanity faces between good and evil will have been decided and cannot be undone. For this reason, Revelation says: 'It is the number of a human being.'[6]

We can also view the number 666 as a measure of time, which renders the history of humanity transparent in a very revealing way. According to Steiner, the anti-Christian powers mounted tremendous attacks on humanity in the seventh and fourteenth centuries, and will do so again towards the end of the twentieth century in 1998, which is three times 666.

The first two attacks I have discussed in my book *The Temple and the Grail* and don't intend to discuss them further here. The third attack began in 1933 when Hitler and the Nazi party came to power in Germany. Despite Hitler's defeat at the end of the Second World War, this attack has nevertheless increased in strength and effectiveness. We might think of the Hydra, the many-headed monster from Greek mythology, who for each head that was cut off grew two more in its place. This imaginative picture is clearly being demonstrated in the crisis of humanity today.

The Book of Revelation is the key book of our time. The path of initiation, which is at the same time the path of development for all of humanity, places us today before the threshold to a new, higher consciousness. In a certain respect we are already in the process, mostly unconsciously, of crossing this threshold.

The powers of evil, which never sleep, are doubling their activity. They try to distract human beings from spiritual reality, from the search for the Grail, for which so many people are feeling the deepest need.

Knowing that we still have a tremendous amount of time before we face the irrevocable choice, we might be inclined to sit back and not trouble ourselves too much. But that would be a dangerous error. The future casts its shadow ahead of time. Even if no final decision is yet made, we are still living in a time of decision.

The way to Christ is not a matter that concerns only Christians, or only inhabitants of a particular country or continent. Revelation speaks of 'a great assembly which no one could count, from all peoples and tribes and races and languages. They stood before the throne and the Lamb...' (Rv 7:9). Everyone who is searching for the wellsprings of life, is really seeking the way to Christ. In our time, just as two thousand years ago, this cannot be done without changing our inner disposition. The call of John the Baptist to change our hearts and minds requires us to let go of rigid traditions and dogmas, age-old prejudices and narrow-minded ways of viewing things.

This book is an effort to contribute to this change of inner disposition – incomplete though it may be. But I hope it may be just enough to show things in a new light.

15

Final Reflections

In Dante's *Divine Comedy*, one of the most powerful and moving works of poetry ever written, the central character, the poet himself, makes an arduous journey through hell and up the mountain of purgatory to paradise. In the last canto of 'Paradiso', the third part of the poem, Dante depicts his ascent into the heavenly spheres, where, through the intercession of Mary, the Queen of Heaven, he is allowed to behold the unfathomable light of the divine Trinity:

> O supreme light who rise far above
> Mortal notions, lend my memory
> A little of what then appeared to me,
>
> And give my tongue all the power it needs
> So that a single spark of your glory
> May be transmitted to people in the future.
>   Canto XXXIII 67–72

Dante experiences in the first place the unity of this Eternal Light, but in this supersensible beholding he himself is changed:

It was my sight which was growing stronger
As I was looking; so what looked like one
Worked on me as I myself changed.

In the profundity of the clear substance
Of the deep light, appeared to me three circles
Of three colours and equal circumference;

And the first seemed to be reflected by the second,
As a rainbow by a rainbow, and the third
Seemed like a flame breathed equally from both.
Canto XXXIII 112–20

In these lines Dante brings the secret of the divine Trinity to expression in a certain way. He sees three circles of equal size and three different colours. The three persons of the Trinity are distinguished in their uniqueness as three separate circles, but are of equal size according to their oneness. 'Rainbow by a rainbow' – here Dante expresses the Father–Son relationship; the Son is in a certain respect a rainbow just like the Father.

The fiery character of the third person of the Trinity refers to the Pentecost event when the Holy Spirit appeared as tongues of fire above the heads of the apostles. When Dante says, 'breathed equally from both', he is thinking in terms of the Creed that the Roman Church had adopted, which says that the Holy Spirit proceeds from the Father and the Son.

As the vision intensifies, Dante discerns in the triune circle a human image in which 'the truth I wished for came cleaving my mind'. When he wants to understand how this image becomes one with the circle, he has a 'high imagination':

At this point high imagination failed;

But already my desire and my will
Were being turned like a wheel, all at one speed,
By the love which moves the sun and the other stars.
Canto XXXIII 142–45

The Beatific Vision, with which the *Divine Comedy* ends, was given to humanity seven hundred years ago to keep alive the memory of our heavenly origin. In our time, however, the way to this threefold vision must be different from Dante's time. Not the Beatific Vision, but true insight into the human being here on earth could, in my opinion, be an adequate starting point for our approach to the Trinity and thus to the mystery of Christ.

This requires further explanation. Over the last two thousand years people have gradually separated themselves from their original, inwardly experienced connection with the spiritual world. A threefold break with reality has occurred, initially only in human thinking, but increasingly in our time in the life of feeling and will.

First, there is the break in our connection with nature. We exploit and destroy nature, but its living essence escapes us because we know only its material aspect. I call this the break with the Father because nature, meaning in the broadest sense the whole visible universe, can be considered as the expression of the ground of existence. We could say that in it lives the sleeping original fatherly will of creation.

Second, there is a break in the 'horizontal' connection between human beings. At levels of society, we witness separation, conflict, abuse of power, self-interest and lovelessness. People are crying out for human connection, ardently longing for it, because the instinctive connections have been broken. Now everything must be laboriously brought about through conscious deliberation. But precisely because of this excess of consciousness, people have become antisocial – a vicious cycle that is hard to break.

Here lies the break with the Son, who, as the brother of humanity, wants to work in human encounters and the unfolding of destiny in such a way that the splintering of humanity can be overcome.

Finally, there is a break with the world 'above' us, the divine or spiritual world. This break is the break of ignorance, of the denial of the spirit, which inhibits the full awakening of the free human being.

The other side of the coin, however, shows the positive result of this development. Human beings have found themselves as individuals. Each of them is an I. As their connection with the threefold reality broke, self-consciousness grew stronger, along with the realisation of being a freely thinking individual.

It is striking that this development at the same time evokes such strong counterforces. The I must be severely tested if it is to unfold its full strength. There are enormously strong forces in our civilization that, on the one hand, want to weaken the human I and alienate it from the earth and, on the other, want to harden it and bind it to the earth.

All forms of vague mysticism and spiritual idealism that avoid clear and exact thinking cause human beings to lose themselves in an alluring surrogate of humanness. The I-experience is enchanted by a make-believe spirituality that is tempting because it demands no effort and puts our thinking to sleep.

We also see the opposite of this in which the human I is dragged down by materialistic prejudices or flattened by bureaucracy and banality. This is the realm of stalwart, no-nonsense individuals. In them the I exhibits a certain, rigid strength, but this is an illusory strength. At its foundation is a very great fear of life.

It is good to examine the feeling of your own I, which is not the same thing as going on a self-indulgent ego trip. The little word I is peculiar in that you can only use it to indicate yourself. No one can call me I; I can only do that myself. This simple consideration can become a profound experience: I am an I. Here I touch upon what is totally my own, inalienable and inescapable, for I am not my father's I nor my mother's I, but my own I, unique in all eternity. It is what is most lonely and, at the same time, what is all-encompassing in me. I am free and sovereign in myself.

But this sovereign feeling of self is not as great a triumph as it perhaps first seems to be, for as soon as I want to meet the world, the other, and receive it into myself, I realise that I am isolated. It is as if everything around me has turned its back on me: nature, human beings, heaven. The bond with the world that I felt as a child now seems thoroughly lost. Perhaps I must first find something in myself that will make the world turn around and show me a face that enables me to communicate with it. That 'something in myself' is concealed within my own I-experience, which can help me find again that which I have lost.

I realise that my self-consciousness has no fullness in it; it is a zero point. But perhaps it turns out to be a point of strength, something like a grain of seed, from which the fullness of the world, and with it the bond with the essence of this world, can arise again. For together with the awareness of the zero point, the realisation of my indestructibility and uniqueness is also present: I enter into the hidden sanctuary within me.

For the Hebrew people the unpronounceable name of God was indicated with the word I. Out of the burning bush Moses heard the words with which the Godhead made itself known to him: *eyeh asher eyeh*, 'I am the I am.' Although my I is not one with God, it is a reflection of the divine in me. You might also say that the I is of the same nature and essence as the divine, just as a drop of seawater is not the same as the sea, but nevertheless is of the same nature, the same substance.

Out of this innermost sanctuary in me, I must find the connection with threefold reality. But this connection cannot be a theoretical matter. It has to be an I-experience, a form of self-knowledge that is more intensive than what we are used to calling knowledge, and which therefore leads to an experience, or to a new kind of believing.

In some way, my I has to be rooted in what I call the ground of creation. The fact that we connect this original ground of things with the Father principle may come from tradition; the name does not matter at this point. Imagine that my I was not rooted in the ground of creation, then my existence would be arbitrary and essentially meaningless. But to begin with, I don't know what this rooting is like. So here I meet the first big difficulty on my path of self-knowledge.

I only become conscious of myself as an I because I am burdened with a material body. My consciousness is extinguished the moment I fall asleep. It is possible that during sleep my I is in a condition of being one with the undivided life of creation, but I am oblivious to that. When I wake up I do sometimes have the feeling of returning from an all-encompassing state into the narrowness of my earthly existence, but this feeling is rare and vague. As soon as I am conscious of myself, I identify not with that all-encompassing condition but with my body. Even then, what lies at the foundations of my body and all of nature is hidden from my conscious I by a thick veil, like the veil of Isis. And when I turn to science to help me lift this veil, I discover not the living divinity, but a stack of blind, mechanical laws that irrevocably bring death.

In this way, I can view nature only as something perishable, and when I identify my body as part of nature, my self-consciousness becomes so bound to the idea of perishability, that I sense a strong paradox concerning the feeling of eternity that my I-experience gives me. Out of my everyday self-consciousness I can make no connection with the ground of creation. If I don't overcome the feeling of transience, of death, which rises out of my body like a kind of illness, I remain in a certain sense outside that aspect of reality that I have called the Father.

For now, I turn away from it and let the feeling of impotence that arises from this inner situation ripen in me. I don't try to suppress it, but rather experience it in all its sharpness.

Meeting the second break is particularly a question of feeling. It is not about being rooted in a ground, but a contemplation of human beings living together in society. From the spatial aspect we come to the aspect of time. Our life unfolds in time as an expression of our destiny. This often appears opaque and seems to consist of a string of accidental happenings. But close investigation can show us that we ourselves are our destiny. Although it looks as if it just happens to us, we meet ourselves through what occurs to us. Our experience of destiny is also an I-experience.

Encounters with other people are of crucial significance in this. Living together means sharing a common destiny. This may involve close connections, such as those we have with parents, siblings, friends, life partners, children and so on, or more distant ones or very brief ones. There is great wisdom in destiny, even when it brings bitter experiences. It is infinitely complicated, but if we ask ourselves what the real point in human destiny is, the reply is very simple: compassion, love and selflessness.

If there is spiritual leadership, a wise Godhead or Lord of Destiny for the individual human being and humanity as a whole, this leadership will certainly be concerned with the development of compassion arising out of a free I, which can deepen to a shared will through the destiny encounters with other human beings.

How little do I manage to do this. How strongly do I experience here also the impotence that prevents me from being compassionate and selfless. Here it is not so much the realisation of transience that keeps me separated from my fellow human beings, but the awareness of moral imperfection – even if this is in the end also connected with our mortality, with our being bound to matter.

From there I come to the question of what is there in the experience of my I that liberates me from these hindrances? What in me overcomes the impotence that is connected with the reality of death? The answer can only be my encounter with the vanquisher of death, Christ himself. Christ does not preach morality but practices it. He shows the highest worthiness of the self by total unselfishness. His sacrificial death bestows on me the resurrection experience. My self-transcending I experiences the spirit as the force of rebirth.

However, this force does not come from myself; it is bestowed on me from out of a higher world.

I find in the wisdom of my destiny the working of a divine power that leads me to death, but in this way seeks to heal me and make me whole. Christ as the Lord of Destiny teaches me the secret of the phoenix that dies and is reborn out of its ashes. He can do this because he has himself passed through death and overcome it through his resurrection. In him wholeness is not broken; as healer and saviour he can bring us again to wholeness.

So that this happens in freedom, so that the human I is not lost in the sea of its divinity and loses all will and insight of its own, Christ sends the Holy Spirit, the spirit of truth, who makes us free. I can live and die in Christ, and again and again return through the spirit to the earth, where I learn to perfect the deficiencies of my being that shackle me to death.

Because the spirit of truth overcomes death – which is really ignorance of the life of the spirit – I can also heal the break with nature. Science, which does indeed lift the veil of Isis, but thus only reveals death, must itself be healed by the spirit. In the perishable human body, I can find the principle of threefoldness through spiritual science, a science healed by the spirit. This vision of the threefold human being, called Anthroposophia, forms the foundation of a modern 'super-natural knowledge' such as Simone Weil was seeking, but did not find before her early death. It is this supernatural or supersensible knowledge that reveals the mysteries of Christianity, as I have tried to demonstrate in this book.

Notes

1. Faith, Knowledge and the Need for a New Revelation

1. The saying is attributed, probably unjustifiably, to the Roman Church Father Tertullian (*c.* 160–240).
2. For a description of the path of inner development laid out by Rudolf Steiner see *How to Know Higher Worlds.*
3. See, for example, Steiner, *The Sun Mystery,* lecture of April 14, 1922, p. 98.

2. What Preceded Christianity?

1. Lesher (trans.), *Xenophanes of Colophon: Fragments,* Fragment 23.
2. Steiner, *Christianity as Mystical Fact,* p. 14.
3. Concerning the existence of a 'pre-Christian' Christianity, St Augustine wrote: 'What is now called the Christian religion existed already among the ancients and was not lacking at the very beginnings of the human race. When Christ appeared in the flesh, the true religion already in existence received the name of Christian.' Quoted in Steiner, *Christianity as Mystical Fact,* p. 118.
4. Heraclitus (*c.* 535–475 BC), pre-Socratic philosopher from Ephesus in Asia Minor.
5. Plato (*c.* 428–348 BC), Greek philosopher and founder of the Academy in Athens (*c.* 387 BC), where subjects such as biology, astronomy, mathematics and history were taught. The Academy is considered the first institution of higher learning in the West. Aristotle studied there for twenty years before founding his own school called The Lyceum.

6. Socrates (*c.* 470–399 BC), Greek philosopher and teacher of Plato. Socrates was accused of dishonoring the gods and corrupting young people and was condemned to death by the court in Athens. He died by drinking hemlock.
7. Philo Judaeus (25 BC – AD 40) was a Hellenistic Jewish philosopher who was born in Alexandria in Egypt.
8. See Vermes, *The Complete Dead Sea Scrolls in English.*
9. King Alexander Jannaeus (*c.* 130–76 BC) was the second king of the Hasmonean dynasty who ruled over the kingdom of Judaea from *c.* 103 to 76 BC. His cruel and oppressive reign was characterised by conflict and bloody civil war.
10. See Steiner, *The Gospel of St Matthew,* lecture of Sep 4, 1910.

3. Mystery Wisdom and the Gospels

1. See Steiner, *How to Know Higher Worlds,* Ch, 9: The Division of the Personality in During Spiritual Training.
2. The four animals were depicted with wings and were sometimes combined: a lion or a bull with a human head, for example, which indicated the high spiritual sphere from which this primal image originated. In Ancient Greek, when earthly intelligence was beginning to awaken, people experienced such imaginative Sphinx-like 'beings', which were connected to an older consciousness, as threatening. The Sphinx devoured those who were unable to solve its riddle: what walks on four legs in the morning, two in the afternoon, and three in the evening? Oedipus, the son of the King of Thebes and an initiate who could be viewed as a representative of the awakening intellect, knew the answer: the human being.

4. Jesus of Nazareth

1. Homer, *The Odyssey,* Book 11, line 558, p. 265.
2. Herod (37– *c.* 4 BC) king of Judea, Idumea, Samaria, and Galilee, was an obscure and very ambitious ruler, who owed his position to the Romans.
3. Heliopolis, the ancient Egyptian city of On in the north of Egypt, was the centre of the Sun mysteries. Moses most likely received his Egyptian initiation there.

4. Steiner, *An Outline of Esoteric Science,* Ch. 4: Man and the Evolution of the World.
5. Whereas many religious traditions speak of a single power of evil, Steiner often spoke about the dual nature of evil and its chief representatives, Lucifer and Ahriman, the Persian name for Satan. Lucifer tempts humanity to pride, egotism and unruly passions, whereas Ahriman tempts humanity to laziness, greed and the denial of the spirit. Instead of vanquishing them, however, we must learn to bring them into balance through the power of Christ.
6. In 597 BC the Babylonian king Nebuchadnezzar conquered Jerusalem and sent the Jewish people into exile in Babylon. This lasted until 537 BC when they were liberated by Cyrus the Great and allowed to return home.
7. Pythagoras (*c.* 580–504 BC) was Greek philosopher from Samos. He travelled often to Egypt and Babylon, where he was initiated, and settled in Croton in the South of Italy. There he founded a wisdom school which was at the same time an esoteric community. He did not leave behind any written scripture but was highly venerated as a great initiate.
8. Beckh, *From the Mysteries.*
9. See Steiner, *The Gospel of St Matthew,* lecture of Sep 2, 1910.
10. Origen (*c.* 185–254) was one of the greatest theologians of early Christianity and a teacher at the Catechetical School in Alexandria. His work was condemned in the sixth century by an Ecumenical Council, especially due to the influence of Roman Emperor, Justinian.
11. Rudolf Steiner describes three sacrificial deeds performed by the Nathan soul prior to the Mystery of Golgotha that prevented certain spiritual powers from overwhelming humanity. On each of these occasions the Nathan soul was permeated by the spirit of Christ. These deeds did not take place on earth but in an adjoining spiritual realm. The mythological images of many peoples – such as Apollo's fight against the dragon – are recollections of these events from a far distant past. See Steiner, *Approaching the Mystery of Golgotha,* lecture of March 5, 1914.
12. According to Rudolf Steiner a nirmanakaya is an astral body that is so highly developed that as it passed through the astral world after death it does not leave behind an unpurified elements.

13. Steiner used the term 'the Fifth Gospel' to refer to the Akashic Record and the results of his spiritual-scientific research that complemented the four canonical gospels.

5. The Fifth Gospel

1. See Steiner, *The Gospel of St John,* lecture of May 31, 1908.
2. Raffaello Santi (1483–1520), known as Raphael, was an Italian painter famous for his paintings of the Madonna and his frescoes in the Vatican in Rome.
3. This was customary in primeval times, especially in Northern Europe. See Steiner, *The Karma of Untruthfulness,* Vol 1, lecture of Dec 24, 1916.
4. The lectures from this cycle form the basis of this chapter.
5. Steiner, *The Fifth Gospel,* p. 56.

6. The Baptism

1. For a more detailed description of the human being as found in anthroposophy, see Steiner, *Occult Science,* Ch. 2: The Nature of Humanity, and *Theosophy,* Ch. 1: The Essential Nature of the Human Being.

7. Signs and Sayings

1. Jethro is also called Reuel in Exodus and Numbers. See Emil Bock, *Moses.*
2. Yahweh is traditionally referred to as a moon god, and just as the moon reflects the light of the sun, so Yahweh reflected the light of the highest sun being, which in the Old Testament is called El-Elyon, the 'Most High God'. See Gn 14:18.
3. *The Epic of Gilgamesh* is a Sumerian-Babylonian story about the hero and ruler of Uruk, Gilgamesh. See also Steiner, *Occult History,* lecture of Dec 27, 1910.
4. Schelling, *The Philosophy of Mythology.*
5. For a more detailed study of the life of Christ from the baptism in the Jordan to the resurrection, see Bock, *The Three Years.*
6. See Steiner, *The Fifth Gospel,* lecture of Oct 6, 1913, pp. 60f.
7. Jn 13:26–28.

8. The scene in which the apostle Peter steps out onto the water to go to Christ only to be overcome by fear and sink down into the waves, is mentioned in Mt 14:28–31.
9. The Sanhedrin was the Jewish Supreme Council, chaired by the high priest and charged with the management of internal Jewish matters. The scribes, the enemies of Jesus, had a great influence in this Council.

8. The Son of Man and the Transfiguration

1. For a more detailed consideration of this term see Steiner, *The Gospel of St Matthew,* lecture of Sep 11, 1910.
2. Steiner, *The Gospel of Matthew,* p. 198.
3. See Steiner, *The Gospel of St Mark,* lecture of Sep 22, 1912.
4. Ibid., lecture of Sep 16, 1912.
5. Bock, *Caesars and Apostles,* pp. 64–75.
6. Ibid., p. 311.

9. The Mystery of Golgotha

1. See Chapter 1, note 1.
2. See Steiner, *The Gospel of St John and Its Relation to the Other Gospels,* lecture of July 7, 1909.
3. See Steiner, *Supersensible Knowledge,* lecture of Oct 25, 1906.
4. Steiner, *The Gospel of St John and Its Relation to the Other Gospels,* p. 272.
5. Ibid.
6. It should be emphasised here that this was a *spiritualised* physical body, the archetype of the physical body that Steiner refers to as the phantom, but without any mineral-physical content. More will be said on this later in the chapter.
7. Steiner, *The Gospel of St Mark,* pp. 130f.
8. See Steiner, *From Jesus to Christ,* lecture of Oct 10, 1911.

10. Ascension and Pentecost

1. This stands in stark contrast to the texts discovered in Nag Hammadi in southern Egypt in 1945, which included translations of original Greek scriptures that had become lost. The stream of

esoteric knowledge contained in these writings contained ancient initiation wisdom and was called gnosis, meaning knowledge. The teachers who occupied themselves with it were called Gnostics. A striking aspect of many of these gnostic texts is that they contain words of the Risen Christ, discussions he is said to have had with his disciples during the forty days between Easter and Ascension. The Coptic manuscript Pistis Sophia, for example, which was discovered much earlier, contains many of these discussions.

2. Steiner, *The Fifth Gospel,* lecture of Oct 2, 1913, pp. 12f.
3. https://en.wikipedia.org/wiki/Veni_Creator_Spiritus.

11. Exoteric and Esoteric Christianity

1. In her book *Fields of Blood,* which looks at religion and the history of violence, Karen Armstrong writes about this development within Christianity: 'It was clearly easier to imperialise the faith than to Christianise the Empire', p. 150.
2. Martin Luther (1483–1546), German priest and theologian. He was excommunicated by Pope Leo X in 1520 after writing his Ninety-Five Theses against the teachings and practices of the Roman Catholic Church in 1517. This is considered, retrospectively, to have launched the Protestant Reformation.
3. John Calvin (1509–64), French theologian, pastor and reformer who lived and worked in Geneva. His doctrine of predestination, the idea that God determined before he created the universe who was to be saved and who damned, is derived from St Augustine.
4. Augustine (354–430), Bishop of Hippo in North Africa and the greatest of the Church Fathers.
5. Rudolf Steiner points to this 'abolition of the spirit' by the Council of Constantinople in 869 as a result of the attack on humanity by the power of the Antichrist. See Steiner, *Michael's Mission,* lecture of Nov 29, 1919.
6. See Steiner, *Supersensible Impulses,* lecture of Oct 1, 1922.
7. This stream was Manichaeism, a Christian Gnostic stream that expanded deep into China as well as to the West. It was founded by Mani or Manes (215–276).
8. Steiner, *Building Stones for an Understanding of the Mystery of Golgotha,* lecture of April 24, 1917, p. 272.

9. See Veltman, *The Temple and the Grail,* Ch. 2: The Mysteries.
10. See Steiner, *The Mysteries of the East and of Christianity.*
11. See Steiner, *Mystery Knowledge and Mystery Centres,* and *Rosicrucianism and Modern Initiation.*
12. The meeting of Paul with Dionysius the Areopagite is described in Ac 17:34.
13. John Scotus Eriugena (815–85), Irish monk, philosopher and teacher at the palace school of Charles the Bald, King of the Franks. His principal work, *De Divisione Naturae,* was declared heretical in the thirteenth century.
14. Charles the Bald (822–77), the grandson of Charlemagne, ruled the western part of his grandfather's empire after it was split into three parts.
15. Robert de Boron wrote, among other things, *Le Roman de l'Estoire du Graal* [Novel of the History of the Grail] which describes the history of Joseph of Arimathea.
16. See Steiner, *Mystery Knowledge and Mystery Centers,* lecture of Dec 9, 1923.
17. The Sassanids ruled from AD 241 to 642. The official religion of the empire was an exoteric form of Zoroastrianism.
18. Genghis Khan (1167–1227). His invincible horsemen conquered practically all of Asia and penetrated deep into Europe.
19. See Steiner, *The Temple Legend.*
20. For a more extensive discussion of this subject, see Veltman, *The Temple and the Grail.*

12. Reincarnation and Karma

1. For a more extensive explanation of subjective and objective guilt see Steiner, *Christ and the Human Soul,* lecture of Oct 13, 1911.
2. Lv 20:10 and Dt 22:22.

13. The Second Coming

1. Jiddu Krishnamurti (1895–1986) later dissolved the Star of the East in 1929, rejecting the role that had been imposed upon him by the Theosophical Society. He went on to become a great spiritual teacher in his own right.
2. See Steiner, *The Reappearance of Christ in the Etheric.*

3. Steiner, *Esoteric Christianity,* lecture of Oct 1, 1911, pp. 82f.
4. Weil, *La connaissance surnaturelle.*
5. Kali Yuga: According to Indian tradition a 'dark' era that lasted five thousand years. Rudolf Steiner confirms this tradition based on his spiritual research and indicates that it lasted from 3101 BC to 1899 AD. 'Dark' means in this connection: cut off from the light of the spirit in human consciousness. See also Steiner, *The Reappearance of Christ in the Etheric.*

14. The Apocalypse

1. For a more in-depth consideration of the Apocalypse, see Steiner, *The Apocalypse of St John.*
2. Visitors to this island in the Aegean Sea can see the cave where John stayed when 'he rose in the spirit' and received his great Revelation.
3. Joachim of Fiore (1132–1202), Italian mystic.
4. Dante Alighieri, (1265–1321), Italian poet, author of *The Divine Comedy.*
5. According to Rudolf Steiner, iron in human blood is the material bearer of the I. Because of the iron content of the blood, the I can be active in the body. The staff is an image of the vertical human form, which is also connected with the indwelling of the I.
6. See Steiner, *The Apocalypse of St John,* lecture June 29, 1908.

Bibliography

Aligheiri, Dante, *The Divine Comedy,* Oxford University Press, UK 1998.

Armstrong, Karen, *Fields of Blood: Religion and the History of Violence,* Bodley Head, UK 2014.

Beckh, Hermann, *From the Mysteries: Genesis – Zarathustra,* Temple Lodge, UK 2020.

Bock, Emil, *Caesars and Apostles: Hellenism, Rome, Judaism,* Floris Books, UK 1998.

—, *Moses: From the Mysteries of Egypt to the Judges of Israel,* Floris Books, UK 2011.

—, *The Three Years: The Life of Christ Between Baptism and Ascension,* Floris Books, UK 1987.

Bowden, Hugh, *Mystery Cults in the Ancient World,* Thames & Hudson, UK 2023.

George, Andrew (trans.), *The Epic of Gilgamesh:The Babylonian Epic Poem and Other Texts in Akkadian and Sumerian,* Penguin Classics, UK 2000.

Homer, *The Odyssey,* Penguin Books, UK 2006.

Lesher, James H. (trans.), *Xenophanes of Colophon: Fragments: A Text and a Translation with a Commentary,* University of Toronto Press, Canada 2001.

Madsen, Jon, *The New Testament,* Floris Books, UK 1994.

Plato, *Timaeus and Critias,* Penguin Classics, UK 2008.

Schelling, Friedrich, *The Philosophy of Mythology,* Spring Publications, USA 2020.

Steiner, Rudolf, *Anthroposophical Leading Thoughts: Anthroposophy as a Path of Knowledge – The Michael Mystery* (CW26), Rudolf Steiner Press, UK 2007.

—, *Approaching the Mystery of Golgotha* (CW152), SteinerBooks, USA 2006.
—, *The Apocalypse of St John: Lectures on the Book of Revelation* (CW104), Anthroposophic Press, USA 1993.
—, *Autobiography: Chapters in the Course of My Life: 1861–1907* (CW28), SteinerBooks, USA 2006.
—, *Christ and the Human Soul: The Meaning of Life – The Spiritual Foundation of Morality – Anthroposophy and Christianity* (CW155), SteinerBooks, USA 2023.
—, *Christianity as Mystical Fact and the Mysteries of Antiquity* (CW8), SteinerBooks, USA 2006.
—, *Building Stones for an Understanding of the Mystery of Golgotha: Human Life in a Cosmic Context* (CW175), Rudolf Steiner Press, UK 2015.
—, *Esoteric Christianity and the Mission of Christian Rosenkreutz* (CW130), Rudolf Steiner Press, UK 2005.
—, *The Fifth Gospel: From the Akashic Record* (CW148), Rudolf Steiner Press, UK 2026.
—, *From Jesus to Christ* (CW131), Rudolf Steiner Press, UK 2024.
—, *The Gospel of St John* (CW103), Anthroposophic Press, USA 1962.
—, *The Gospel of St John and Its Relation to the Other Gospels* (CW112), Anthroposophic Press, USA 1982.
—, *The Gospel of St Luke* (CW114), Rudolf Steiner Press, UK 1988.
—, *The Gospel of St Mark* (CW139), Anthroposophic Press, USA 1986.
—, *The Gospel of St Matthew* (CW123), Rudolf Steiner Press, UK 1985.
—, *The Karma of Untruthfulness,* Vol. 1 (CW173), Rudolf Steiner Press, UK 2005
—, *Knowledge of Higher Worlds: How is it Achieved?* (CW10), Rudolf Steiner Press, UK 2011.
—, *Michael's Mission: Revealing the Essential Secrets of Human Nature* (CW194), Rudolf Steiner Press, UK 2016.
—, *Mysteries of the East and of Christianity* (CW144), Rudolf Steiner Press, UK 1972.
—, *Mystery Knowledge and Mystery Centres* (CW232), Rudolf Steiner Press, UK 2013.
—, *Mystics After Modernism: Discovering the Seeds of a New Science in the Renaissance* (CW7), Anthroposophic Press, USA 2000.

—, *Occult History: Historical Personalities and Events in the Light of Spiritual Science* (CW126), Rudolf Steiner Press, UK 1982.
—, *Occult Science: An Outline* (CW13), Rudolf Steiner Press, UK 2011.
—, *An Outline of Esoteric Science* (CW13), SteinerBooks, USA 1997.
—, *The Philosophy of Freedom* (CW4), Rudolf Steiner Press, UK 2011.
—, *The Reappearance of Christ in the Etheric: A Collection of Lectures on the Second Coming of Christ,* SteinerBooks, USA 2022.
—, *Rosicrucianism and Modern Initiation: Mystery Centres of the Middle Ages – The Easter Festival and the History of the Mysteries* (CW233a), Rudolf Steiner Press, UK 2020.
—, *The Sun Mystery and the Mystery of Death and Resurrection: Exoteric and Esoteric Christianity* (CW211), SteinerBooks, USA 2006.
—, *Supersensible Impulses in the Historical Development of Humanity* (CW216), Rudolf Steiner Press, UK 2024.
—, *Supersensible Knowledge* (CW55), Anthroposophic Press, USA 1987.
—, *The Temple Legend: Freemasonry and Related Occult Movements from the Contents of the Esoteric School* (CW93), Rudolf Steiner Press, UK 2002.
—, *Theosophy: An Introduction to the Supersensible Knowledge of the World and the Destination of Man* (CW9), Rudolf Steiner Press, UK 2011.
Veltman, W. F., *The Temple and the Grail: The Mysteries of the Order of the Templars and the Grail and their Significance for Our Time,* Temple Lodge Publishing, UK 2021.
Vermes, Geza (trans.), *The Complete Dead Sea Scrolls in English,* Penguin Classics, UK 2011.
Weil, Simone, *La connaissance surnaturelle* [Supernatural knowledge], Cactus, France 2024.

Index

www.ingramcontent.com/pod-product-compliance
Ingram Content Group UK Ltd.
Pitfield, Milton Keynes, MK11 3LW, UK
UKHW021915160926
475582UK00003B/100

9 781835 750148